W

THE BEDFORD GROUP TRANSEARCH

...as followed up on his outstanding
Lead Well, with another insight-packed
...lping anyone improve their leadership
...dition to providing evidence-informed
...has partnered with Alan Mulally—prob-
...g CEO on the planet—to provide prac-
...d personal experiences. This spectac-
...duced a book that you won't want to

...**ON,** author of *Positively Energizing*
...and *Practicing Positive Leadership,*
...n Russell Kelly Professor Emeritus
...ment & Organizations, Ross School
...s, and Professor Emeritus of Higher
...School of Education, University of

...egins with great self-leadership. *A Time*
...and effectively conveys this message
...pages. With a compelling foundation
...cience combined with insightful and
...es, this book equips leaders with the
...the what of leadership excellence."
...Group President at Steve Madden,
...ard of Governors at Parsons School

"The world needs better leaders now more than ever! If you are looking to be one of those game-changing leaders, you need a coach. In this book, you get *two*! Craig Dowden and Alan Mulally will coach and guide you through a master course of leadership and life. The lessons in this amazing book will not just make you a better leader, they will make you a better person. Read it. Study it. Live it. You will have no regrets!"

—CHESTER ELTON, Bestselling author of *Leading with Gratitude* and *Anxiety at Work*

"Craig Dowden's newest book is a Masterclass in CEO training, refocusing our attention on the power of mastering our emotions and challenging our fixed mindsets for the improvement of our companies, teams, and ourselves. It's jammed full of amassed advice from industry professionals, delightful stories, and even fun facts (such as that an average airplane has four million parts). It is exactly as billed: an evidence-informed roadmap to help you maximize and realize your potential and become the leader the world needs you to be."

—MICHAEL GARRITY, CEO Financeit

"As an insightful expert on leadership and a trusted advisor to corporate executives, Craig Dowden offers invaluable advice for how leaders can navigate their organizations through our increasingly volatile, uncertain, complex, and ambiguous world. Craig's central message—that leadership begins with mastering ourselves and our environments—is particularly timely as leaders are being called on to stand at the forefront of societal change."

—GOLDY HYDER, CEO Business Council of Canada

"In this inspiring and powerful book, Craig Dowden provides invaluable insight into the key qualities that leaders must master to navigate the challenges and opportunities that lie ahead. Using a combination of scientific research and engaging masterclasses from one of the top CEOs of all time, Craig provides an actionable roadmap for how we can maximize our leadership impact every single day."

> **—FRANCESCA GINO,** Harvard Business School professor, author of *Rebel Talent*, and recognized as one of the world's 50 most influential management thinkers by Thinkers50

"Craig Dowden has crafted another must-read primer for anyone in leadership navigating today's perilous workplace environment. Be prepared to abandon your comfort zone and be reinvigorated through self-reflection so that you're fully prepared to tackle the complexities of employee engagement in today's highly dynamic organizations."

> **—DON ROMANO,** CEO Hyundai Canada

"Craig's relentless passion for bringing out the best in leaders and the teams that they lead is present on every page of this book. Using his powerful and persuasive approach of combining compelling research with actionable practice, *A Time to Lead* provides an invaluable roadmap to any leader who is looking to thrive in the new world of work. I walked away inspired and empowered to be a better leader after reading this book."

> **—DAN TURNER,** CEO Xperigo

"We are living in times where, as leaders, we are having to lead through situations that were unimaginable only a short while ago. Craig provides a path of insightful and actionable approaches to help leaders improve their own potential to lead more effectively."
 –GERRARD SCHMID, former CEO Diebold Nixdorf

"Craig Dowden brings his tremendous humanity combined with solid leadership science from the best-run companies to help navigate these unprecedented times. An incredible executive coach and guide, Craig challenges us with lessons on not just how to be, but also, what to do to master authentic leadership. *A Time to Lead* goes well beyond raising our inspiration and insight—it provides us with a detailed plan to be the best leaders we can be!"
 –SUE HUTCHISON, CEO Equifax Canada

"I have had numerous opportunities to discuss leadership issues and qualities with Craig, both individually and with Craig's CEO Mastermind colleagues, over the past few years. *A Time to Lead* combines the powerhouse duo of Craig with Alan Mulally, former CEO of Ford Motor Company and Boeing. Their mixing of science with extensive leadership experience powerfully outlines the fundamental qualities leaders need in order to be successful at all levels. In reading this book, I have taken many notes and have paused for reflection on how I can incorporate some exciting ideas into my leadership toolbox. A must-read."
 –KEVIN FORD, CEO Calian, CEO of the Year
 Award Winner

"What I love most about *A Time to Lead* is that it showcases not only who you need to be as a leader, but what you need to do as well. Drawing on insightful Masterclasses and thought-provoking research, this remarkable book provides an evidence-based framework for mastering self-leadership. *A Time to Lead* must be included on the top shelf of your leadership library."

—ANDY TAYLOR, CEO Gore Mutual Insurance

"The bar for great leadership has been raised! It is time we step up to the challenge, sharpen our skills, and revisit what leadership is all about—managing ourselves so we can serve our people to accomplish great things. Craig does a masterful job of articulating the fundamental building blocks of leadership excellence while weaving in the personal touch and many insights of legendary CEO Alan Mulally—what a treat! This will be required reading for my leadership team. Well done!"

DREW COLLIER, CEO LGM Financial Inc.

"Leadership has become exponentially harder just in the last few years, and leaders need a reliable playbook to guide them during these challenging times. Craig Dowden brings the most essential aspects of leadership to life with concrete examples and actionable takeaways, providing a valuable guide for our times."

—ADAM BRYANT, managing director The ExCo Group and bestselling author of *The CEO Test: Master the Challenges That Make or Break All Leaders*

"As an exceptional coach and trusted advisor to senior executives, *A Time to Lead* brilliantly captures Craig's passion for the science and practice of effective self-leadership. Drawing on his extensive coaching experience, combined with a solid foundation of compelling research, this book provides inspiration and insight into the evolving landscape of leadership and equips readers with the tools they need to drive their success in the teams and organizations they lead."

–ANNE WHELAN, CEO Seafair Capital.

"In this expertly researched and thought-provoking book, Craig Dowden outlines the leadership qualities that are essential for our success, both as individuals and as organizations. Backed by evidence and enriched by insightful case examples and masterclasses, *A Time to Lead* is a must-read for executives who desire to be at the top of their game. This is a powerful resource you will want to refer to time and again."

–ROB PATERSON, CEO Alterna Savings

"Having spent many hours in virtual conversations with Craig and fellow CEOs during the pandemic, I have experienced firsthand Craig's ability to translate leadership concepts into tangible actions we can take away and implement. He regularly brings together a network of highly accomplished business and academic leaders and the outcome is a masterclass in authentic leadership, which is what his new book delivers. *A Time to Lead: Mastering Your Self…So You Can Master Your World* is an invaluable resource for CEOs and leaders looking to excel."

–KIM FURLONG, CEO Canadian Venture Capital and
Private Equity Association of Canada

"With legendary CEO Alan Mulally providing wonderful insights throughout, Craig Dowden's book *A Time to Lead* is chock-full of relatable, timely, and impactful techniques to help you master the art of leadership. A book well worth your investment in time and application."
   –DAN PONTEFRACT, Leadership strategist and best-selling author of *Lead. Care. Win.*

"We find ourselves leading in a world that will continue to demand the best of us. As leaders, the ability to be personally prepared has never been more important. Craig's understanding of our leadership challenge and his focus on seven areas of mastery provides strong guidance on how we can step up and respond. *A Time to Lead: Mastering Your Self…So You Can Master Your World* helps us understand how to do just that."
   –MIKE WARD, CEO and Chief Sustainability Officer IKEA Canada

"*A Time to Lead* holds excellent advice for leaders navigating volatile times. Self-mastery is, indeed, the foundation of great leadership! Craig Dowden combines science with very practical exercises. He and Alan Mulally show how these principles can produce the results you need."
   –MARILYN GIST, Bestselling author of *The Extraordinary Power of Leader Humility* and Professor Emeritus and former Associate Dean at the Albers School of Business and Economics at Seattle University

"In *A Time to Lead*, Craig Dowden expertly builds an evidence-based business case for the key leadership qualities for today and tomorrow. This compelling book takes the science of leadership excellence and translates it into powerful practice. Craig provides a masterclass on the being and doing of high-level leadership."

–DR. GRAHAM SHER, O.C., CEO Canadian Blood Services and Order of Canada recipient (2021)

A TIME TO
LEAD

A TIME TO LEAD

MASTERING YOUR SELF...
SO YOU CAN MASTER YOUR WORLD

CRAIG DOWDEN, PhD

WITH ALAN MULALLY AND SARAH MCARTHUR

Worth® BOOKS

Print ISBN: 978-1-63763-075-4
E-book ISBN: 978-1-63763-076-1

Cover Design by Bruce Gore, Gore Studio, Inc.
Interior Design and Illustrations by Bill Kersey, KerseyGraphics

Library of Congress Control Number: 2022910583

Foreword

I loved *A Time to Lead*!

Some management and leadership books can be justly criticized for having too much theory and almost no practical "how-to" application, which is needed to illustrate how a "real world" leader can make the theory come to life. Others can be criticized because they present a leadership success story with little of the underpinning theory, which explains why the leader was successful. In putting together *A Time to Lead*, Craig Dowden has successfully captured the best of both worlds. He shares a very comprehensive list of qualities that are essential for the personal development of *any* leader and then provides a "Masterclass" from an amazing leader on how the theory can be used to make a huge positive difference.

In the spirit of full disclosure, I must share my history with Craig's wonderful collaborators, Alan Mulally and Sarah McArthur—both of whom I have known well for over twenty years.

As an executive coach, I have had the privilege of working with over two hundred outstanding CEOs.

My far-from-secret opinion is that Alan Mulally is the greatest corporate leader whom I have ever met. He has developed an incredible and unique process for leadership that I have never seen matched! I have been fortunate enough to have been recognized twice as the #1 Leadership Thinker in the World. Alan Mulally, more so than even Peter Drucker, has been the major source of leadership knowledge for me.

Sarah McArthur, the editor of the award-winning *Leader-to-Leader* journal, is also a brilliant writer and editor who is able to translate the work of great executives and thinkers into language that can be understood and used by leaders at all levels in any type of organization. She also has a deep personal knowledge of Alan's work that comes through clearly in this book.

A Time to Lead is organized around seven critically important, proven elements that are needed for outstanding leadership. Craig skillfully covers each element with just the right amount of detail—enough depth to let the reader know what is needed without overuse of references that can lead more to confusion than to clarity. Each section of the book uses Alan's rich leadership history to illustrate key points and to bring the theory to life. Each element of leadership is integrated into Alan's "Working Together"© Management System theory, which is the most comprehensive and effective process for leadership that I have ever observed. To me, Craig's ability to successfully complete this integration is brilliant!

Here are my suggestions for you, as a reader. Digest each chapter—one at a time. Stop at the end of Craig's section on each element and reflect on what it means in the context of your own leadership journey. Then slowly take in each of Alan's Masterclasses. Learn from his incredible success and then translate what you have learned from Alan into your own life.

To use myself as an example, I have incorporated what I learned from Alan's Business Plan Review process into my own coaching. I have successfully piloted a two-year Life Plan Review (LPR) process with fifty great leaders (the LPR process is described in my *New York Times* bestselling book *The Earned Life*). The LPR has also been used by hundreds of my fellow coaches. In the same way, you can use what you learn from Alan, Craig, and Sarah in almost any aspect of your life from coaching to personal growth to family. Take this valuable information and experiment by applying what you learn in your own life!

Along with being one of the best leaders in history, Alan Mulally is also an incredibly generous man. I have had many opportunities to observe Alan teaching leaders from around the world. Many of these leaders have benefited from his teachings—some have not. The leaders who implemented Alan's concepts became more effective. Not surprisingly, the leaders who just listened to the words stayed the same. Everything taught in this book works. It doesn't "kind of" work, or "sort of" work, or only work in this or that situation. *It works!* If *you* implement the concepts taught in *A Time to Lead,* not only will you become a better leader, you will also become a better person.

Craig, Alan, and Sarah have written a very thoughtful and practical book that will help you become a more effective leader if:

▶ You have the *courage* to look in the mirror and honestly assess yourself—comparing what you have learned to your present leadership behavior.

▶ You have the *humility* to admit that you can always improve and dedicate yourself to the continuous learning suggested in this book.

▶ You have the *discipline* to do the work required to make it happen.

The final chapter of *A Time to Lead* is fittingly called "A Challenge." This is my challenge to you: do whatever it takes to implement what you learn from Craig, Alan, and Sarah into your own life!

Marshall Goldsmith
Executive educator and coach,
two-time Thinkers 50 #1 Leadership Thinker
in the World, award-winning speaker,
and multiple New York Times bestselling author

TABLE OF CONTENTS

An Invitation 21

Meet Your Co-pilot 33

CHAPTER 1: **Mastering Our Mindset** 51

CHAPTER 2: **Mastering Our Emotions** 77

CHAPTER 3: **Mastering Our Resilience** 101

CHAPTER 4: **Mastering Our Strengths** 121

CHAPTER 5: **Mastering Receiving Feedback** 139

CHAPTER 6: **Mastering Difficult Conversations** 161

CHAPTER 7: **Mastering Authentic Leadership** 189

A Challenge 213

Acknowledgments 221

Meet My Collaborators 227

Notes 231

AN INVITATION

Has there ever been a more complex time to lead? Being a leader has never been easy. Today the responsibility is even more daunting. Now more than ever, strong leadership is not only about a burgeoning bottom line; it is about respecting and taking care of multiple stakeholders. Our employees, our shareholders, our communities will accept nothing less.

Leaders today are expected to take positions on more than just their market strategy or operational efficiencies. They must think about and share openly what they are doing to protect and enhance the well-being of those around them. For their employees, this is not just limited to providing fair wages and career advancement. It is about supporting and nourishing the "whole person." And it doesn't stop there.

Leaders are also being asked to take a stand on environmental, social, and governance (ESG) issues.[1] They must actively lead their organizations with an eye toward equity, diversity, and inclusion. They face demands about how they are using artificial intelligence. What causes do they support? What clients will they work with (or not)? And then there's COVID-19! The questions are endless, and everything is under a laser-powered microscope.

Leaders are expected to use their voice to speak to things that were never a part of their role, even a short time ago. With so many competing interests, invariably there will be consequences, no matter their course of action. Leadership is not for the faint of heart. Nor should it be.

WE ARE LIVING IN A VUCA WORLD

The acronym *VUCA* was created to frame the state of our world, and it becomes more relevant every day. It has been accurately described as a catch-all expression to capture the idea, "It's crazy out there!" VUCA stands for:

▶ **Volatility:** This relates to the speed of change. How quickly is the market, industry, or world evolving? The faster the rate of change, the higher the volatility.

▶ **Uncertainty:** This refers to our level of confidence in predicting the future. How confident are we in terms of anticipating where things are going?

▶ **Complexity:** This captures the number of factors that are simultaneously operating to affect an outcome. The more factors to consider, the more complex the environment.

▶ **Ambiguity:** To what extent do we have complete information? Is the available information contradictory? Our answers to these questions provide an index of the level of ambiguity.

Very few people would argue against the applicability of these core concepts to the compound challenges of twenty-first-century leadership. It is also difficult to imagine how our world will not become more "VUCA-fied" as we move forward.

A special mention needs to be made about the impacts of uncertainty and ambiguity, which affect human beings in profoundly negative ways. One influential study demonstrated that we would rather receive news about the worst-case scenario today than wait to potentially receive better news in the future. Essentially, waiting for a better outcome is more painful than receiving the worst news right away.[2] Let that sink in for a moment! Leaders need to address this innately human reality in their employees, shareholders, customers, and communities. Although it is no easy feat, leaders must also navigate and manage their own psychological tendencies to react in this way.

Has there ever been a more important time to lead? More than two decades of experience as an executive coach has shown me that, despite these obstacles, there is tremendous potential. Leaders can effect profound, positive change in the world around them. This era is calling for an advanced and more humanistic approach to leadership, which requires exceptional self-insight and self-management. It demands us to be at our best every single day. While the road is uncertain and rocky, the rewards—both personally and professionally—are beyond measure for those of us who are up to the challenge.

WHAT A TIME TO LEAD!

When I wrote my first book, *Do Good to Lead Well: The Science and Practice of Positive Leadership*, I saw a world in which there was an inherent conflict within leaders about whether doing good would contribute to their success. They understandably wondered about the consequences of doing the right thing. They questioned whether it was sufficient for achieving their personal and collective goals or if it would just slow them down or even get in the way.

In *Do Good to Lead Well*, I presented six pillars of positive leadership: self-awareness, civility, humility, focus on the positive, meaning/purpose, and empathy. These pillars were based on the prevailing and long-standing science of leadership, team, and organizational excellence. The evidence was overwhelming that *doing good* was not counter to *leading well*. In fact, it was necessary.

Ironically, the final piece of writing my first book was also the most challenging. Although this may surprise you, the hardest part was creating the title. Nothing seemed quite right. I couldn't come up with anything that captured the core themes. Although I am very happy with the title *Do Good to Lead Well*, the journey wasn't easy.

For this book, the opposite occurred. The title immediately sprang to mind based on my work with top leaders in some of the world's most-recognized organizations. I also have the pleasure of supporting others who have built tremendous companies and legacies. Although some of these may be lesser known in the public eye, they are no less successful. Through my work, I have talked and collaborated with the most accomplished thought leaders, bestselling authors, and TED speakers in the world.

Over the course of my conversations with these exceptional individuals, one consistent message has held true: to successfully navigate the new terrain of leadership, we need to be at our best. To be clear, this goes well beyond managing balance sheets, product lines, and operational requirements more effectively. Although necessary, these are insufficient to thrive in our current environment.

We need to possess an advanced level of under-standing about the inner workings of our minds *and* our hearts. We must be acutely aware of our strengths and our derailers. We need to recognize our potential blind spots and how they may contribute to the pitfalls along the way. Without focusing on self-mastery every day, we cannot achieve our potential or the potential of those we lead.

A TIME TO LEAD

You must put on your own mask before
you can assist other passengers.

— AIRPLANE TRUISM

The purpose of this book is about mastering the inner game of leadership. As in *Do Good to Lead Well*, the primary foundation on which my arguments will be built are the social, leadership, and behavioral sciences. We cannot afford to ignore the powerful, evidence-informed insights that are readily available. Otherwise, we run the risk of stepping on our own rakes and causing tremendous harm to ourselves and those we care about most.

At the same time, I am acutely aware that the applicability of the research to the "real world" is commonly questioned. Critics argue that the evidence has been generated in an ivory tower and not relevant to Wall Street. Recognizing this, I am thrilled that Alan Mulally, former CEO of Ford Motor Company and of Boeing, will help me provide you with Masterclasses throughout this book.

Alan is one of the world's most widely accomplished and respected CEOs of all time. He will personally attest to the power of the leadership qualities in this book and will show you in intimate detail how you can capitalize on their power in your organization, just as he did while at the helm of two of the greatest companies in the world. I cannot think of a more credible advocate for making the case for these leadership qualities than Alan.

Whether you are a start-up founder, a junior or senior executive, or aspiring to these positions, this book provides an evidence-informed roadmap to help you maximize and realize your potential and become the leader the world needs you to be. Here is what I will cover:

Meet Your Co-Pilot, Alan Mulally

First, I will introduce you to your Masterclass instructor, Alan Mulally. You will hear the highlights of his extraordinary career and the key inflection points that led him to the corner office of two global powerhouses. You will also obtain deeper insight into his "Working Together" Management System, which was the foundation of the tremendous success he experienced as a chief executive and led to his being profiled in the bestselling book *American Icon*.

In each chapter, we will provide a Masterclass on how Alan's "Working Together" Management System relates to the leadership quality under investigation. The goal is to give you privileged access to one of the top CEOs in our history and understand how he leads by "Working Together."

Chapter 1: Mastering Our Mindset

Leadership starts with our mindset. How we look at the world heavily impacts our experiences and outcomes. To effectively lead, we must be aware of and adjust our mindset constantly. Otherwise we may miss invaluable information in our personal and professional environment. We may not capitalize on opportunities or we may fail to learn from our setbacks. We will start our journey by examining the secrets to mastering our mindset and learn how this directly applies to our leadership effectiveness. We will learn about ground-breaking research into the power of mindset and understand how we can leverage these key insights.

Chapter 2: Mastering Our Emotions

An equally important element for effective leadership is mastering our emotions. We are constantly bombarded with new information, challenges, and interpersonal conflicts. To stay steady and remain calm require extraordinary emotional self-awareness and intelligence. If we become "emotionally hijacked," it can be virtually impossible to perform at our best or inspire others to perform at theirs.

This chapter examines the *what*, the *how*, and the *why* of emotions when it comes to leadership. We will learn the science and practice of emotional self-management. Through developing a deeper understanding of our own emotional journey, we are better equipped to support those around us.

Chapter 3: Mastering Our Resilience

Building personal, team, and organizational resilience is a critical competency for any aspiring or current leader. It is an extension and specialized application of mastering our emotions. It is a muscle we must consciously and deliberately exercise every day.

This chapter explores the science and practice of resilient leadership. We will look at why pressure and stress are not the same thing and how this distinction unlocks the code to maximizing our resilience. We will discover how our relationship with stress plays a major role in determining our level of resilience as well as our ability to enhance or weaken resilience in others. We will also explore several evidence-based steps we can take to expand our resilience tool kit.

Chapter 4: Mastering Our Strengths

To be successful, it is imperative that we understand where we add the most value. On the best teams, players understand, accept, and fulfill their roles. Being a leader is no different. This chapter explores the science and psychology of strengths. We will learn how to identify our special gifts and how to use this insight to maximize our own potential.

This level of awareness is invaluable when it comes to building our teams as well as hiring and retaining the right talent. By leveraging the best within and around us, we put ourselves in the best position for success.

Chapter 5: Mastering Receiving Feedback

Although bestselling author Ken Blanchard famously claimed that feedback is the breakfast of champions,[3] very few people seem anxious to sit down for the meal, let alone enjoy it. A major stumbling block is that every one of us has blind spots and triggers that get in the way. To realize our potential, we need constructive and honest feedback from the people around us. How can we possibly know where we add the most value if we don't receive that input? How can we identify where we can make positive changes in our approach to drive greater impact? Feedback is rocket fuel for self-mastery, especially when it comes to leadership.

Chapter 6: Mastering Difficult Conversations

Many people find it challenging to engage in difficult conversations. Being a leader is no exception. The difference is that we are routinely put in situations where we need to have more of them. Unfortunately, many leaders feel poorly equipped, which drives them to avoid, delay, or fumble through these types of interactions.

This chapter will define what a difficult conversation is and the reasons why it is so challenging to navigate. The chapter will conclude with evidence-based strategies we can use to successfully prepare for and engage in these important conversations.

this book. The motivation behind this approach was to show that these leadership qualities directly led to success on the biggest stage and readily apply in the most complex organizations in the world.

I love it when things come together. And boy, did they ever.

AN AMERICAN ICON

I am thrilled to introduce your CEO Masterclass instructor, Alan Mulally. I cannot think of anyone more qualified than Alan to be your co-pilot on your leadership journey based on his list of extraordinary accomplishments. He is a shining example of the core idea in this book: leadership excellence is not only about who you need to *be* as a leader; what you need to *do* is equally important.

I was extremely fortunate to meet Alan during my book-writing process. And to begin with simply the facts of his leadership service journey, here's what I learned: Alan started his career with Boeing commercial airplanes immediately following his graduation from the University of Kansas, where he earned bachelor's and master's degrees in aeronautical and astronautical engineering.

He had the honor to serve in the design, production, and support of every Boeing airplane, including the 707, the 727, the 737, the 757, the 767, and the 777, where he played the role of chief engineer and program manager.

Chapter 7: Mastering Authentic Leadership

While the deeply personal nature of exploring one's authentic leadership can make the topic uncomfortable territory for most leaders, scientific and anecdotal evidence paint a different picture. Rather than take away from our power, authentic leadership enhances it. As opposed to driving people away, being true to who we are brings people closer because they know what to expect when they interact with us. We must be clear on who we are as a leader and what is most important to us to pursue our goals with passion and purpose. This chapter will delve into the soul of leadership and challenge us to look *inward* to foster our impact *outward*.

A Challenge

This final chapter will take stock of the journey we made together and reflect on the key lessons from the CEO Masterclasses and other resources provided throughout this book. It will also point the way forward and shed light on what we need to do to fully embrace our *Time to Lead*. I will close with a challenge to stretch out of your comfort zone and to strive for the potential within you. It's about energizing us to be at our best and providing a roadmap for our pursuit of excellence, both individually and collectively.

AN INVITATION TO LEAD

There you have it. I have laid out the journey ahead and what will be required of you. My hope is that this book will test and challenge some of your assumptions and beliefs about leadership and how to get the best out of ourselves and the people we lead.

I can't think of a more inspiring way to start our journey together than by introducing you to your Masterclass instructor, Alan Mulally.

MEET YOUR CO-PILOT

If you learn to work together with others, you're going to be able to make a big difference for the people of our world.
—ALAN MULALLY

Critics often argue that leadership books provide idealistic and unrealistic advice that does not apply in the "real world." People question whether this utopian view of leadership can truly be implemented, especially in the rough and tumble world of stock prices, corporate boards, and international markets.

When I was thinking about the framework for *A Time to Lead*, there were two core ideas I wanted to implement throughout the book. First and foremost, I wanted each chapter to include a CEO Masterclass that exemplified the leadership quality being discussed. The goal of the Masterclass was to provide a real-life example of the quality in action.

The other core idea was to profile an extraordinary CEO who exemplified each of the qualities outlined in

When he was CEO, he had the chance to launch the 787 Dreamliner.

Alan told me he never imagined he would leave Boeing until he received an unexpected call from Bill Ford, the great-grandson of Henry Ford, who wanted Alan to join Ford Motor Company as CEO. While it was a transformative call, it may surprise you how it unfolded.

Alan recalls, "The more of the situation Bill shared with me, the more difficult the story got, and the more I wanted to hear about this important company."

Here were just some of the headwinds facing Alan if he took the job:

▶ Ford had become a house of brands through their acquisitions of Aston Martin, Jaguar Land Rover, Volvo, and Mazda. While 80 percent of its business was still with the Ford line, Ford had lost its way in terms of "who it was and what it looked like as a brand."

▶ The company was losing money on all its brands and vehicles. Alan says, "As Bill explained, our cost structure was not competitive." In fact, the first forecast Alan saw showed a $17 billion loss, which indeed occurred four months later.

▶ The company had become very regionalized, which resulted in little synergy in working together worldwide. This was a critical issue because it ran counter to Henry Ford's vision to operate in every country where he sold vehicles "so the company could provide not only great vehicles, jobs, and careers, but also support the economies around the world."

"Working Together" was the hallmark of Alan's success at Boeing and given the challenges Ford was facing, this is what made him a perfect fit to lead Ford.

Understandably, Alan was initially reluctant to take the job and even declined. He had never wanted to leave Boeing. What changed his mind, he says, was that, with this opportunity, "I felt like I was being asked to serve a second American and global icon, and I couldn't pass that up."

A testament to Alan's character and unwavering belief in the importance and potential of working together is that when Bill offered him the opportunity to be both chairman of the board as well as CEO, rather than take the expanded role, Alan said to Bill, "You are being so honest, transparent, and authentic about the situation, and this is essential for turning Ford around. What we are going to have to do will require us working together, so I'll only come if you stay on as Chairman."

Thus, from September 2006 through June 2014, Alan served as president and chief executive officer of the Ford Motor Company and as a member of Ford's board of directors. He led Ford's transformation into one of the world's leading automobile companies and the number-one automobile brand in the

United States. He guided Ford in working together on a compelling vision, comprehensive strategy, and relentless implementation of the One Ford plan to deliver profitable growth for all the company's stakeholders.

Ford went from losing $17 billion on its automotive operations in Alan's first year to profitability in his third year. During the global financial crisis of 2008, with industry giants such as GM and Chrysler going bankrupt, Ford was the only automotive company not to receive a bailout from the US government. Here are some other notable achievements:

▶ Ford's stock price increased by over *1,800 percent* during Alan's tenure, moving from an intraday low of $1.01 in 2006 to $18.37 in 2014.

▶ Despite this extraordinary turnaround, Alan shared that this pales in comparison to his proudest accomplishment: "The most important performance measure of all was employee satisfaction. Our engagement scores were around 40 percent when I started, which, as you know, is the average score for most companies around the world. When I left eight years later, our employee satisfaction was at 92 percent, the highest of any company at that time."

This leads to a powerful question—how on earth did he do this?

"WORKING TOGETHER" MANAGEMENT SYSTEM: PRINCIPLES AND PRACTICES

Alan has created and perfected the stakeholder-centered "Working Together" Management System over a lifetime of service to two of the world's most recognizable brands. He has applied its principles and practices to fuel his management system in driving exceptional growth and orchestrating tremendous turnarounds. Here are the principles and practices:

Our "Working Together" Principles and Practices

CULTURE SKILLED AND MOTIVATED TEAMS

- People first...Love 'em up ♥
- Everyone is included
- Compelling vision, comprehensive strategy, and relentless implementation
- Clear performance goals
- One plan
- Facts and data

- Everyone knows the plan, the status, and areas that need special attention
- Propose a plan, positive, "find-a-way" attitude
- Respect, listen, help, and appreciate each other
- Emotional resilience–trust the process
- Have fun–enjoy the journey and each other

Profitable Growth For All (PGA) ♥

People First...Love 'em Up

According to Alan, at Boeing this was surrogate for, "These are wonderful, talented human beings who are committing their lives to creating a new airplane. This is a phenomenal undertaking. An average airplane has around four million parts. Just think about the quality, the reliability, the efficiency, the safety, the systems engineering, and the maintainability that it takes to create one of these airplanes. These airplanes are probably the most sophisticated products in the world that transport anywhere from two hundred to three hundred people halfway around the world. It's incredible, and it's very important that we acknowledge and recognize this by putting our skilled and motivated people first and loving them up."

Applying this to your own organization, the products or service may change, but the principle of putting people first and loving them up does not.

Everyone Is Included

This philosophy is not some meaningless exaggeration designed to inspire false hope. For Alan, this literally means *everybody*: "It's all of the communities in which we operate because what we are doing is creating value for all of our stakeholders, and they need to be part of the team every step of the way. Our stakeholders include our customers, our employees, our suppliers, our governments and communities around the world, and our bankers and investors."

Compelling Vision, Comprehensive Strategy, and Relentless Implementation

A great example of this practice comes from Alan's career with Boeing. "We had a compelling vision for every airplane we built, which we created by answering questions like, Is this airplane going to be short-range or long-range? Is it going to be point-to-point, nonstop service?"

Alan continues, "Once you have created the compelling vision, the next step is building the comprehensive strategy for achieving it. This includes not only the technical strategy but also the people strategy, the working together strategy, the partnership strategy, and the financial strategy."

A critical component of strategy and a consistent theme across "Working Together" is that everyone needs to know all the elements of the strategy and the plan to achieve it.

The last step, relentless implementation, garnered the most press and skyrocketed Alan to the top of his craft, leading to his being profiled in the bestselling book *American Icon: Alan Mulally and the Fight to Save Ford Motor Company* by Bryce Hoffman.

The backbone of relentless implementation is the Business Plan Review (BPR). This meeting was held on the same day, time, and location every week, without fail. Alan states, "Every stakeholder participated, and attendees went through every element of the vision, strategy, and plan. They looked for areas that were going well as well as issues that needed special attention."

Clear Performance Goals

A hallmark of these meetings was that everyone knew what was expected of them and reported their status to the group. The extent to which they were on plan was represented by a color-coded system. Not surprisingly, the chosen colors were green, yellow, and red, and the following definitions apply to any team utilizing the BPR process:

- ▶ **Green = All systems go.** That element of the plan is on schedule, with clear roads (or skies) ahead.
- ▶ **Yellow = Caution.** Although there are concerns with this element of the plan, we have an idea or ideas about what is causing the issue and have identified possible fixes.
- ▶ **Red = A new issue that needs a solution.** We consider these "gems," and the entire team works together to find a solution to turn the reds to yellows to greens.

One Plan

The power of the BPR emanates from its focus on the One Plan. Every stakeholder is working on the same plan, which leads to maximum alignment. People know exactly what is expected of them and how their work contributes to the overall vision for the company. This is incredibly powerful from both a motivational and performance perspective.

As Alan explains, "Most companies have many plans, and everybody's wondering what the plan actually is." This abundance of plans leads to division as leaders tend toward a myopic focus on their specific area of the business rather than having a more holistic view. It also leads to mismatching priorities, as divisions without knowledge and awareness of the impact of what other divisions are doing can feel their work is more important. This can lead to infighting and competition for resources. This environment is the antithesis of "Working Together" because it interferes with maximizing our collective potential.

Facts and Data

Alan notes that while a foundational principle and practice of "Working Together" is caring about what people think, the work must be rooted in objectivity.

"Although we want to know what people think," he says, "we also want to know what facts and data they are looking at to draw those conclusions. This is really important because when we take action, we want to move forward with confidence, knowing that we are using the best data to inform the most appropriate action to solve the issues at hand."

Everyone Knows the Plan, the Status, and Areas That Need Special Attention

The existence of the One Plan and the transparency with which it is handled during the weekly BPR meetings mean that everyone has a clear line of sight into what is happening in the company and their role for accomplishing it.

If you think this would never work in a large, multi-national organization, think again. Remember, this was successfully implemented in both Boeing and Ford, two of the largest and most complex organizations in the world!

This also means everyone knows *every* part of the plan. It is not limited to the technical and operational issues. It includes fully detailed financials as well.

One of the key outputs of the BPR meetings is the seamless ability to identify areas that required special attention. These were the red-light status updates, which were assigned to Special Attention Meetings. At Special Attention Meetings, people would come together to identify possible solutions to the issues at hand. This allowed for immediate and constructive action to address the top areas of concern in the One Plan.

Propose a Plan, Positive, "Find-a-Way" Attitude

The culture throughout "Working Together" is all about exhibiting a positive, "find-a-way" attitude.

Alan notes, "This one always makes me think of the Henry Ford quote, 'Whether you think you can, or you think you can't, you're probably right.'"

Being positive and having a "find-a-way" attitude doesn't mean you avoid dealing with the reality of the situation. It means that you inspire and challenge people to propose ways of working together to turn the reds to yellows to greens.

Respect, Listen to, Help, and Appreciate Each Other

"The way we treat each other is essential to being a smart, healthy, and successful organization. The "Working Together" principles and practices create a psychologically safe environment, and respecting, listening, helping, and appreciating one another are how we do this," says Alan.

Emotional Resilience—Trust the Process

"This is an innovative and creative process. We expect the unexpected and expect to deal with it," says Alan. "In practice, emotional resilience is about how quickly you recover from a setback, and it is also another manifestation of the positive attitude. We trust the process of "Working Together" because we know that we have a system in place to identify potential risks as well as insights into where we need to prioritize our attention and our energy. This empowers us because we know what the situation is that we are facing, and together we can find the best solution possible."

Have Fun—Enjoy the Journey and Each Other

Last, but not least, it is essential to "enjoy the journey and each other. We find joy in the process of "Working Together," and we inspire the best in ourselves and in those we lead.

"I still wake up every day and say 'thank you,' says Alan. "Thank you for the honor to serve two American and global icons and all the people of our world with the very best cars, trucks, and airplanes that offer safe and efficient transportation. Thank you to all the thousands of people that I've had the pleasure to work and serve with."

"WORKING TOGETHER" MANAGEMENT SYSTEM

Our "Working Together" Management System

The "Working Together" Management System power-fully captures *who you need to be* as a leader and *what you need to do* to achieve extraordinary success. Its principles and practices provide a reliable operating process and outline expected behaviors for all the stakeholders to work together to adapt and thrive in a rapidly changing world.

It is important to reinforce the last point. The stake-holder-centered "Working Together" Management System includes all the stakeholders. Everyone involved is expected to participate, follow, and nurture all the elements of "Working Together," including the oper-ating processes and expected behaviors. The collec-tive goal is to create and deliver value for all the stake-holders and the greater good.

The diagram shown on page 45 the five elements of the "Working Together" Management System: principles and practices, governance, leadership teams, creating a value roadmap, and a business plan review. It's important to note that these five elements are interdependent. Although separately each one provides a piece of the puzzle, as Aristotle famously surmised, "The whole is greater than the sum of its parts." Let's discuss each one in turn.

Principles and Practices

As you can see from the the preceding diagram, the Principles and Practices are the foundation of "Working Together," which is why they are at the top of the graphic. They supersede everything. While "Working Together" is tremendously powerful, it cannot operate to its highest level without relentlessly following the Principles and Practices just described. As Alan notes, "They enable talented and motivated people to join together and work together to deliver a compelling vision together. And they create a smart and healthy organization culture with clear operating processes and expected behaviors for all the participants and stakeholders."

Governance

The governance process relates to how we manage ourselves in every element in the system. According to Alan, "It includes our stakeholders, our board of directors, our leadership team, our creating value roadmap, and our business plan review meetings where we review our vision, strategy, and plan and where we identify the areas of our plan that need special attention. The governance process also extends to the special attention meetings, where we work the issues and develop our better plan."

Leadership Team

The leadership team process uses a simple matrix organization to enable and facilitate "Working Together" between the business units and the functional skill teams. "Our stakeholder-centered leadership team includes and represents all our stakeholders: customers, employees, suppliers, unions, bankers, investors, governments, and communities around the world."

Creating Value Roadmap

The Creating Value Roadmap process unites everyone to develop the vision, strategy, and plan. The ultimate goal is to build and implement a business plan that creates near- and long-term value for everyone. Alan explains, "The Creating Value Roadmap process is also designed to regularly review our progress using our Business Plan Review meetings to identify the areas of our plan that need our special attention. It is important to note that all our stakeholders are participating in and contributing to our Creating Value Roadmap process."

Business Plan Review

The Business Plan Review (BPR) is the weekly review of the business environment, vision, strategy, plan, and our better plan going forward. In every BPR, our leadership team reviews the entire business plan and the status and forecast against each one of its elements.

Alan says, "Our objective is that by the end of the meeting, everyone on the team and all our stakeholders know where we are individually and collectively in implementing our plan and what areas of our plan need our individual and collective special attention."

The updated BPR information is shared with all the stakeholders.

Final Thoughts

What I love about the "Working Together" Management System is the heart in the middle—Profitable Growth for All (PGA). Its foundation is built on love, humility, and service. You can easily see what makes this approach unique and extraordinarily effective.

A TIME TO LEAD AND A TIME FOR "WORKING TOGETHER"

You can see why Alan is the ideal co-pilot for this leadership journey. His "Working Together" Management System has not only sparked exceptional results but has also been applied within the largest and most complex organizations in the world. He has rich, varied, and hands-on experience seeing the impact of these qualities on both the financial results and employee engagement.

In each chapter, I will share segments of our conversation that relate to the specific leadership quality in question. These will be presented in the corresponding CEO Masterclass. The purpose of these Masterclasses is to demonstrate how the leadership qualities I present in this book have contributed to the success of one of the most highly regarded CEOs of all time and impacted two of the most renowned companies in the world. Their purpose is also to show that these leadership qualities apply in any organization regardless of size, industry, or complexity.

Let's start with the foundational leadership quality of Mastering Our Mindset.

MASTERING OUR MINDSET

*The hand you are dealt is just the
starting point for development.*

—CAROL DWECK[4]

Early on, I asked Alan whether the leadership qualities I will be covering in *A Time to Lead* are important to his "Working Together" Management System.

"They are foundational," he replied, "and leadership starts with your mindset."

This is a powerful observation, and it maps perfectly with my own experience coaching executives. Before we can effectively lead others, we must effectively lead ourselves. If we fail to understand and adjust our views of the world and the people within it, we run the risk of undermining our own success and the people we lead.

While it is a relatively widespread belief that you cannot teach an old dog new tricks, science tells a different story. We as human beings have a tremendous capacity to learn throughout our lifetimes. One of the fundamentals of learning is both appreciating and understanding the power of mindset.

We will start our journey by understanding the science of mindset before learning how we can become more masterful in its application.

THE SCIENCE OF MINDSET

Let's start with a common example of how our mindset not only affects how we process information but also impacts our experiences. Imagine you're getting ready for an upcoming meeting and are thinking, *This is going to be torturous and a complete waste of time.* Guess how the meeting turns out? What are the chances you'll be right?

This is a concrete example of the power of mindset. When we feel certain about a particular outcome, we scan our environment for confirmatory evidence. When we "know" this will be an awful meeting, we look for data that validates our initial judgment.

A common application of this phenomenon with which you may already be familiar comes from the field of medicine: the placebo effect.[5] This occurs when a patient believes they are receiving medication when in fact they are not. However, despite the nonmedicinal properties of the placebo (in many cases, it is a sugar pill), many patients respond in the same way as if they had received a drug. Patients *expect* to feel relief, and they do.

The power of our mindset can be observed in lots of everyday situations. In 2008, researchers from the California Institute of Technology and Stanford University studied how the taste of wine was directly affected by its price.[6] Twenty volunteers were told the prices ranged from $5 to $90 per bottle. Then the participants tasted the wines while having a functional magnetic resonance imaging (fMRI) scan. "The subjects consistently reported that they liked the taste of the $90 bottle better than the $5 one, and the $45 bottle better than the $35 one."[7]

What was fascinating about this study was that the effects of the prices were not just limited to how participants reported experiencing the taste of the wines. The fMRI scans revealed that they also experienced more activity levels in the "brain region that is involved in our experience of pleasure."[8] The impact was both psychological *and* physiological!

One final example of the placebo effect comes from Medical Students' Syndrome (MSS), a phenomenon that was first reported in the 1960s. MSS is a psychological condition among medical trainees who experience the symptoms of the disease or diseases they are studying.

Although you may be thinking this syndrome is limited to medical students, think about a time when you did not feel well and decided to visit several reputable health-related websites to figure out what was wrong. How did that turn out?

For many, as they read the possible reasons for their symptoms, they start thinking they have far worse diseases and complications. They even consider racing to the hospital, a phenomenon termed *cyberchondria*.

It's important to note that nothing about our objective circumstances has changed. We still have the same "symptoms" as before. What has shifted is our mindset. One brief visit to a website changed everything. Now we are making new connections and drawing conclusions based on our interpretations of the information we are receiving. What was seen as mildly uncomfortable before is now seen as potentially life-threatening.

Application to Leadership

Unpacking these examples has striking insights to offer in terms of how our mindset profoundly affects our ability to engage in effective self-leadership. Do we see a situation as a problem or an opportunity? Do we look for what could make something possible, or do we immediately dismiss it as impossible? Depending on the questions we ask ourselves, our sources for answers will be markedly different.

You can also readily see how our mindset can affect how we view our employees, our organizations, and our stakeholders. It also readily affects the emotions we experience and the choices we make. The data we focus on necessarily shifts our perspective in these different situations. As leaders, we can *fall victim to* or *be bolstered by* our mindset.

FIXED VERSUS GROWTH MINDSET

Every individual, team, and organization is searching for a competitive advantage. With so much information available and with so many variables to juggle, it makes sense that words such as *agile*, *adaptable*, and *flexible* take center stage in any discussion of leadership.

To be an effective leader, it is essential to elevate our awareness of our current mindset, to change it when appropriate, and to recognize how our mindset affects not only ourselves but the people around us.

Given this, it is not surprising that the provocative and groundbreaking work of Stanford professor Carol Dweck, one of the most highly respected psychologists in the world, captured the attention and imagination of corporate audiences and business leaders.[9] Although her original research focused on children, it's become an integral part of leadership development because of its relevance and seamless application.

The primary thesis of her research is that human beings occupy one of two mindsets at any given moment: *fixed* or *growth*. The fundamental difference between these mindsets is their prevailing belief about the possibility of change. Those with a fixed mindset believe our potential and ability to learn is stagnant. There is nowhere to go from here; if we can't do something today, it means we will not be able to do it tomorrow.

A growth mindset, however, looks at our potential as much more dynamic. Given the right degree of focus and practice, we can significantly move the needle in any area we choose. If I struggle with something today, I can take proactive and powerful steps to change things tomorrow.

Simply put, with a fixed mindset, we can't get off the ground. With a growth mindset, the sky is the limit.

Not surprisingly, our mindsets have direct implications when it comes to how we respond to various situations. Figure 1 outlines some common examples.

FIGURE 1: SUMMARY OF FIXED VERSUS GROWTH MINDSET REACTIONS

	Fixed	Growth
Challenges	Avoid	Embrace
Setbacks	Give up	Persevere
Effort	Pointless	Work hard
Critical feedback	Deflect/ignore/lash out	Learn
Success of others	Threat/ignore	Learn/celebrate

Let's take a closer look at each of these situations and how you might respond in either a fixed or growth mindset.

Challenges

According to Dweck, when we are in a fixed mindset, our primary objective is to look smart. Her research showed that participants with a fixed mindset "prefer tasks they can already do well and avoid ones in which they may make mistakes."[10] If this is our default reaction, it is little wonder that the presence of a challenge tends to prompt an avoidance strategy. Why would we take on a challenge when it could reveal our incompetence? If we fail, it will definitively show that we are in over our heads.

When interviewed by the *Atlantic*, Dweck explained that her research with graduate students showed that those with a fixed mindset "saw challenges as risky. They could fail, and their basic abilities would be called into question."[11]

You can readily see how this mindset would cause leaders to play it safe and do things the way they have always been done. They would resist the need for change. They would double down on what worked in the past. In today's VUCA world, this is a recipe for disaster.

Adopting a growth mindset when we are faced with a challenge prompts an entirely different reaction. Rather than feeling intimidated or motivated to avoid it, we feel energized about the opportunity. Challenges present an exciting opportunity to test the upper limits of our potential. They provide incredible insight into our current level of performance. Last but not least, they give us an invaluable chance to learn and grow through the experience. We can take the lessons learned, both positive and negative, and apply them so we can be even better the next time. Challenges are embraced as a crucial part of our personal and professional development.

Setbacks

Life, personally and professionally, inevitably comes with setbacks. They are unavoidable. For a leader with a fixed mindset, the first sign of trouble or resistance is a signal to give up. If the early returns do not look promising, they abandon ship. Dweck points out that when graduate students "hit obstacles, setbacks, or criticism, this was just more proof that they didn't have the abilities they cherished."[12]

However, when we have a growth mindset, we are much more expansive in our thinking. For example, when leaders with a growth mindset face a setback, it is a puzzle to figure out rather than an insurmountable obstacle to overcome. They take the time to examine the situation from multiple angles and look for what they can learn from the experience.

Effort

This is likely the most straightforward application of the two mindsets. If I truly believe I cannot change for the better, then putting in more effort is a waste of energy and time. It will not affect the outcome.

For a growth mindset, effort is the fuel that drives the engine of peak performance. I am most concerned about whether I gave it my all. Did I leave anything on the table? That is the only way to know for sure whether this is an untenable situation.

Critical Feedback

Feedback is a natural part of life.[13] For a leader, this tendency is even more amplified. We are in a position where we regularly obtain feedback from our employees, our supervisors, our customers, and our stakeholders. Some of it can be quite critical in nature. How we receive feedback is widely influenced by our mindset.

If we are in fixed mode, our overriding desire to look smart will likely make us feel attacked or defensive. Our fixed mindset denies or deflects the criticism and wants to ignore it. Unfortunately, when we employ these tactics, we miss an invaluable opportunity to learn, because we believe there's nothing wrong or "it's not my problem."

When we are in a growth mindset, feedback is like eating our vegetables. Even if it doesn't taste great, we recognize and accept it is good for us. It makes us healthier and stronger. We have more energy to tackle our everyday challenges. The parallels with leadership are varied and valid.

Success of Others

Some leaders can feel quite threatened when their employees succeed. They may be inclined to take the credit or minimize their expressions of gratitude or recognition toward these individuals. They may feel concerned that their authority is compromised when people on their team are doing well.

This is no small matter—and employees know it. A study conducted by Office Team revealed some striking numbers:[14]

▶ Two-thirds of employees indicated they would "likely leave their job if they didn't feel appreciated," which marked a significant increase from 51 percent in 2012.

▶ The data is even more troubling when it comes to millennials, three-quarters (76 percent) of whom say they would leave their jobs if they didn't feel appreciated. Given that millennials are becoming the largest generation in our workforce, the implications are stark.

▶ More than half of all managers (54 percent) say it is common for staff to quit due to a lack of recognition.

Although expressing appreciation does not take much time or effort, the results are profound.

When leaders adopt a growth mindset to the success of their team members, they will not hold back recognition and appreciation. Even better, they will be more inclined to "spread the wealth" and try to pair up team members so that they learn from each other's successes. They will also encourage sharing and celebrating achievements within their teams, which is a hallmark of maximum engagement. Rather than a threat, we can see the success of others as a motivation to pursue our own success.

Approaching this situation from a growth mindset also allows us to see the upside of others' successes. When the team looks good, the leader looks good. As the expression goes, a rising tide lifts all boats. When our team succeeds, we will get noticed. Our team members will talk about how amazing it is to work for us. Engagement will likely skyrocket. To be successful as a leader, we must make those around us better. This is the core idea Marshall Goldsmith brilliantly captured in the title of his bestselling book on leadership, *What Got You Here Won't Get You There*. Fostering and celebrating others' successes exemplify true leadership success.

BARRIERS TO A GROWTH MINDSET

Like many things in life, the popularity of Dweck's mindset research has led to some misconceptions and misapplications of the concept. This prompted her to write an article for *Harvard Business Review* with the apropos title "What Having a 'Growth Mindset' Actually Means,"[15] in which she highlighted three important misconceptions about a growth mindset.

Misconception #1: "I already have it, and I always have."

One of the most dangerous assumptions we can make is that a fixed mindset is only the unfortunate domain of other, less-enlightened individuals. So if you read the previous section with the utmost confidence that you have benefited from a growth mindset your whole life and will continue to do so, this warning is especially for you.

Dweck points out that "a 'pure' growth mindset doesn't exist, which we have to acknowledge in order to attain the benefits we seek." This is an important revelation because it highlights the fact that we can slide in and out of a growth mindset. If we assume we will constantly be in growth mode, that in itself is a fixed mindset statement. It denotes permanence. It refuses to accept the possibility that we could change.

The critical takeaway here is to recognize what factors can trigger a fixed or growth mindset. The more aware we are of our mindset at any given moment, the more empowered we are to address it.

Misconception #2: "A growth mindset is just about praising and rewarding effort."

Although effort is a critical differentiator of a growth mindset, it is not the be-all and end-all. Outcomes are also vitally important. If we fail to recognize how our efforts are translating to our results, we can miss extraordinary opportunities for learning.

Dweck advises that we need to focus on both effort and outcome to achieve the full benefits of a growth mindset. If we focus solely on effort, we can be wasting energy and time pursuing a suboptimal course of action. It can also interfere with us "seeking help from others, trying new strategies, and capitalizing on setbacks to move forward effectively."[16]

Misconception #3: "Just espouse a growth mindset, and good things will happen."

This is another perilous pathway. Everything in life does not always work out as planned. Sometimes you can do all the right things and still get a suboptimal or even negative outcome. In other cases, we can do everything wrong and still achieve a positive result. Sometimes life doesn't work out the way it should.

Nowhere is this more evident than when it comes to innovation and risk-taking. In some circumstances, leaders can do all the market research and have sufficient resources (financial and human) for a project, and things will still go off the rails. Failure is a necessary part of innovation.

While espousing a growth mindset maximizes the chances of a positive outcome, it doesn't guarantee one.

RECOGNIZING OUR FIXED-MINDSET VOICE

One of the primary things we need to be aware of when it comes to our mindset is our self-talk. This inner dialogue has a profound and often unrecognized impact on us. Learning to recognize our fixed-mindset voice and how to pivot into a more growth-oriented frame of mind is incredibly important.

The first step is awareness. It lies with identifying what Dweck terms our inner Fixed Mindset Voice,[17] which is unique to every one of us. It's a voice in our head that repeats negative statements to keep us entrenched in that mindset. Although it isn't always easy to identify that voice, it is important to recognize what it sounds like when we hear it so we can take steps to counteract it. Here are a couple of quick examples to show this process in action.

Example #1

Fixed-Mindset Voice: "I am never going to figure this out."

Analysis: There are several reasons why this is problematic.

First, the statement is phrased from an identity perspective, "I am." This denotes it is a part of *who we are* versus *what we are doing*. Being mindful of the permanence of the label used is critical.

Second, by saying *never*, we are using an absolute term to describe our situation. Be mindful of how often and when you use expressions such as *never* and *always*. If we are "never" going to figure this out, what are the chances that we will? How much effort do you think we will put into doing so? Again, these are the hallmarks of a fixed mindset.

Reframe for Growth: Rather than say, "I am never going to figure this out," use other approaches. For example, ask yourself several different questions: *What am I missing? What are some possible sources of support for this challenge? Who do I know who may be able to help me with this? What advice would I give to someone who was in the same situation?*

You can also use more growth-oriented statements such as, *"This may take some effort/time," "I will need to stay focused to figure this out,"* or *"This will be a good test of my limits/patience/skills."*

All these questions and statements assist us in proceeding with more of a growth mindset.

Example #2

Fixed-Mindset Voice: "I wish I were more like Anne/Joe. I wish I didn't have so much bad luck. I can't seem to escape it."

Analysis: As you may have picked up from the first example, these are self-limiting statements. They indicate a gap without any acknowledgment of how to fill it. When framing the issue this way, there is no path forward.

An equally, if not more, problematic aspect of this phrasing is that it places the responsibility *outside* of ourselves. There are external reasons for our current results (e.g., Anne/Joe is more talented, or I am an unlucky person). This means it is not my fault and I cannot do anything to change my situation.

Reframe for Growth: When reframing for growth, ask yourself, *What can I learn from Joe in terms of how he approaches similar situations I am facing? How might I engage Anne to be a mentor/reference source as I am making my career decisions? What steps did they take to get to where they are?*

Reframing your approach through questions unlocks multiple paths forward. It empowers us to see there are numerous possibilities to explore. Rather than seeing things as a finite end point, we are at the beginning of our exploration journey.

DON'T LET YOUR SUCCESSES TRICK YOU INTO A FIXED MINDSET

Although much has been made about how a fixed mindset can negatively impact our successes, our successes can also put us at risk of adopting a fixed mindset. The corporate landscape is filled with examples of companies and industries that failed to learn from the successes of their rivals. You do not need to look any further than well-worn examples such as Blockbuster, Kodak, Nokia, and BlackBerry. The fixed mindset of these companies serves more as an end-of-days warning of a dystopic future. As Dweck explains,

"When we have a fixed mindset, our success can make us feel impenetrable."[18]

What's notable is that in each of these case examples, the company doubled down on what initially made it successful. They refused to listen to feedback from the market and their employees. They felt they knew better. Unfortunately, these companies provide countless lessons of what *not* to do.

However, there is a shining example from a globally recognized brand that beautifully illustrates the power of shifting from a fixed to a growth mindset. This company is 170 years old and was seen as one of the world's most trusted businesses. It was built on a reputation of precision, impartiality, and exceptionalism. Do you know the brand? You might have a subscription.

The organization I'm speaking of is the *New York Times*.[19]

When Mark Thompson took the helm in 2012, the *Times* was in relative freefall. Despite being one of the world's most recognized and respected news organizations, it was hemorrhaging significant market share and their digital subscriptions, despite their reputation, were not only weak but waning. Their long history made it more difficult to change course. Their philosophy and practices reflected a fixed mindset.

In particular, they were dismissive of market feedback and the success of other start-ups such as *Huffington Post* (now *HuffPost*) and *Buzzfeed*.

They felt they had it all figured out. The company's inaction made a clear statement: "Why do we need to change? We are the best in the world!" Mark Thompson recognized that the *Times* needed to break that type of mindset.

"After we first talked about the future of journalism and how we were going to reach out to broader audiences, we needed a significant change in leadership across the organization. Consumer behavior's changing, the competitive landscape's changing, the relationship with the major digital platforms—it's like some vast series of complicated weather systems crashing into one another. All of that requires responsiveness by the organization and requires change. Adaptability and flexibility become important."[20]

This quote is indeed a perfect illustration of a growth mindset in action. It is *future-oriented* as opposed to looking to the past. The *Times* finally asked itself, *What do we need to learn to stay relevant and successful in the future?*

Here are other concrete and powerful ways the *Times* shifted its thinking from fixed to growth:

▶ **Challenges:** They moved away from legacy thinking (e.g., we are just a newspaper business) to expanding their overall vision (e.g., we are a global content creation company in which print distribution is one of our platforms).

▶ **Critical Feedback:** For a long time, the *New York Times* was resistant to criticism of their model, especially when they were compared to upstarts such as *Huffington Post* and *Buzzfeed*. They stopped turning a blind eye to this feedback and embraced it as an opportunity to evolve and thrive in the new world.

▶ **Success of Others:** Rather than downplay or dismiss the success of the "new kids on the block," the *Times* decided to look at what lessons could be learned and how they could capitalize on their existing strengths to overcome these relatively new and increasingly powerful rivals.

This shift in mindset had a significant impact on the bottom line. The following graph showcases the

New York Times **Company Price**

share price over time during Thompson's leadership tenure. Even though the environment was the same, reframing their mindset and approach revitalized the company and brought it back to being an industry leader, not just in terms of reputation but in financial performance as well.

THE POWER OF REFRAMING

One of the biggest challenges for CEOs is effectively managing their board of directors. Most boards consist of six to ten members. A large one might include twelve to fifteen people. Your job is to provide a quarterly snapshot to these extremely accomplished and intelligent individuals about everything that is going on in your business and to be prepared to discuss these issues in great detail when requested.

Now imagine that, rather than having a "normal" board, you have forty members to whom you report. For many people, this might seem overwhelming and incredibly intimidating. How can you possibly manage this impressive and highly diverse group?

This was the scenario facing Kim Furlong, CEO of the Canadian Venture Capital and Private Equity Association (CVCA). When we spoke, she provided a shining example of the power of mindset.

Let's start with what she didn't do: adopt a fixed mindset. If she had approached this situation with a fixed mindset, she likely would have seen the terrain as wrought with danger. She likely would have avoided the members of the board and asked herself questions such as, *How could I possibly engage with everyone? How will I ever be able to deliver a convincing presentation, because someone will always find a problem or concern with what I'm talking about?* Those negative thoughts and feelings would have quickly multiplied and likely undermined or even crippled her performance when it mattered most.

You may be wondering how Kim approached this situation. How could she possibly adopt a growth mindset when faced with such overwhelming odds? Great question.

Rather than see these forty incredibly accomplished board members as threats to her success, she viewed them as a bounty of expertise, experience, and support. As opposed to seeing them as enemies, she viewed them as allies. She rightly believed everyone at that boardroom table wanted the CVCA to be the best it could be.

Armed with that mantra, she reaches out to board members on a regular basis. She asks them what keeps them up at night. What are their concerns? How can she provide them with advance information? She does not avoid them at all costs.

She creates maximum opportunities for engagement, which build mutual trust and respect.

You could apply this example to countless others in leadership. The next time you are tempted to view your situation through a fixed mindset, think of Kim. You'll be glad you did.

REFRAMING FAILURE

Failure should be our teacher, not our undertaker. Failure is delay, not defeat. It is a temporary detour, not a dead end. Failure is something we can avoid only by saying nothing, doing nothing, and being nothing.

—DENIS WAITLEY

Although there are many famous quotes on failure, this one is arguably my favorite because it exemplifies failure from a growth mindset. Rather than viewing failure as something that defeats us, it recognizes that failure is a necessary part of growth. Unfortunately, despite its importance, we tend to have a dysfunctional relationship with failure. There's a notion of permanency in that we feel we will always fail, so why bother to keep trying? However, failure, if we let it, can be a wonderful teacher.

As leaders, we need to be more accepting of failure—for ourselves and for our teams. Failure happens to everyone. When pursuing any goal, let alone one that stretches us, we need to recognize we won't be perfect right from the start. If you're learning to ice skate, are you going to skate perfectly as soon as you step on the ice? Of course not. There will be many struggles, missteps, and falls. If we think of our next fall as being one step closer to success, we are more motivated to continue. We focus on gains rather than losses. We look at advancements rather than setbacks. When our minds approach failure in this way, we are more energized to persevere.

When we look at famous quotes by Albert Einstein ("It's not that I'm so smart, it's just that I stay with problems longer") and Thomas Edison ("I have not failed. I've just found 10,000 ways that won't work"), we can see that they embraced challenges. That's the very definition of a growth mindset. They weren't discouraged by the possible failures; they welcomed them as necessary companions on the road to success. To maximize our potential, we must take a growth mindset to move forward, recognizing not only the possibility but the value of failure.

By adopting a growth mindset, we believe things can eventually work out. So instead of avoiding a challenge, staying in the same spot, or quitting after we encounter a few setbacks, we choose a different path forward. A growth mindset keeps us curious rather than afraid. It keeps us going. We shift course and continue moving ahead.

CEO MASTERCLASS WITH ALAN MULALLY: ON MASTERING OUR MINDSET

The quality of our mindset is intricately and intimately connected with the quality of our results as well as the quality of our relationships. Indeed, the notion of a growth mindset permeates throughout the "Working Together" Management System.

At the heart of "Working Together" is PGA—Profitable Growth for All. As Alan notes, "How can we get the best out of everyone if we don't all benefit from our efforts? We are more inspired when we feel that we are a part of something that matters. A large part of making that happen is through individual and collective growth."

A growth mindset is an integral part of the leadership team. Every member has a development plan, which they openly share with each other. This is incredibly powerful because it signals that we all have areas for improvement and that successful personal and professional change is a team sport. None of us can achieve excellence alone. Continuous improvement requires input and support from everyone around us.

The idea of a growth mindset also applies in "Working Together." "Many people get to a place where they are comfortable with where they are, and it's not easy for them to change and grow. The 'Working Together' Management System challenges you to focus on the things that help you further execute the plan and mitigate possible risks. In this context, a growth mindset is absolutely key, because you're not only solving today's problems but you're also creating and executing an even better plan to solve the problems of tomorrow."

There is no better place where this is exemplified than during the Business Plan Review, where the end goal is moving from red to yellow to green. Each week, every stakeholder presents their status updates with an eye for either keeping things on target or course correcting in areas that require attention.

Within the "Working Together" framework, there are several leadership beliefs, values, and behaviors that tie everything together. Leaders are not only expected to be role models in this regard but must hold others responsible for their commitments as well. This creates an enduring system of accountability: to self and to others. Several key beliefs, values, and behaviors relate to the growth mindset:

- Coach/Develop Others: Leaders are expected to coach their teams and their fellow leaders to maximize their potential.
- Continuous Improvement: We continually search for ways to be better.
- Lifelong Learning: We never stop learning, and we have a responsibility to ourselves, as well as to each other, to approach things with this type of growth mindset.

All of these taken together provide an extraordinary recipe for success. "By design, the system pushes you into a growth mindset. What's equally important is that you have a process that supports its continued application, and everyone is included. How awesome is that?"

CONCLUDING THOUGHTS

Leadership starts with our mindset. It is essential for us to recognize how we are viewing the world at any given moment because it has profound implications for what we see. In particular, our mindset can lead us to capitalize or miss out on opportunities in the environment. It may contribute to our failing to learn from failure. Paying special attention to our mindset and ensuring we stay in growth mode is key to our success and will inspire those around us to follow our lead.

CHAPTER 2

MASTERING OUR EMOTIONS

*Emotion can be the enemy, if you give into
your emotion, you lose yourself. You must
be at one with your emotions, because
the body always follows the mind.*

—BRUCE LEE

Although most executives lead with their head, an equally important aspect of leadership is mastering our emotions. Our emotions continuously impact our personal and professional lives; thus, staying in control of our emotional state is a vital leadership skill. Rather than being at the whim of our emotions, how can we see them more objectively so we can use the information they're providing us without becoming totally off-balance? Learning this skill is much easier said than done.

In any given situation, positive or negative, we are at risk of our emotions getting the better of us—undermining our relationships and overall success. If we do not effectively manage our emotions, how can we possibly make good decisions as a leader? How can we inspire others to follow our lead if we do not appear to be able to control ourselves?

Emotions are an important guide, but when we allow them to take over, it is virtually impossible to realize our potential. This chapter explores our emotional management system by providing evidence-informed insights to interpret and manage our emotions more effectively and stay focused during the most critical times.

THE GENESIS AND PURPOSE OF EMOTIONS

As simple as it may sound at first, defining what an emotion actually is can be surprisingly difficult.[21] The American Psychological Association defines emotion as "a complex reaction pattern . . . by which an individual attempts to deal with a personally significant matter or event."[22]

Within the context of this definition, you can already see why this is such a complex issue; what is "personally significant" varies widely from one person to the next. When we apply our own definition of significance to someone else's situation, we are inviting trouble. Furthermore, if we do not keep our emotions in check, they can quickly undermine our effectiveness as leaders if we make a mountain out of a molehill. People who observe our overreaction, including our employees, will likely lose confidence in our leadership.

Essentially, emotions are data points. They are invaluable internal sources of information, which give us a sense of how we are doing in any given moment. As such, we need to be masterful at deciphering the messages they are trying to convey.

When we experience positive emotions, we might say we "feel good" about what is currently happening. What we are doing and saying "feels right." It suggests a sense of convergence and alignment.

Negative emotions, however, represent our early warning system. Our feelings are telling us something is not right. They are asking us to pay attention to some aspect(s) of our lives and letting us know something needs to be addressed. While that request can start out lower in intensity, it can quickly escalate if we fail to listen to our internal detection system.

Both kinds of emotions are valuable. We should not prefer or seek out one over the other. They are telling us a story, and all this information is vital to our personal and professional success.

BECOME AN EMOTIONAL DETECTIVE
WHEN IT COMES TO OUR EMOTIONS

One of the biggest obstacles we face when it comes to mastering our emotions is how we react when they emerge. Unfortunately, we can quickly judge our emotions and immediately start to wonder whether we have any right to feel what we feel, especially if we feel our reaction is irrational. This can create a negative spiral that inhibits learning and prolongs frustration. This is similar in form and function to our fixed-mindset voice taking over our internal conversation relating to our emotions.

Whenever my clients ask, "Should I be feeling like this?" about a particular issue, I always say *yes*! That is our right as human beings. At the same time, there is also a great responsibility attached because even though we have the right to feel this way, we must sit with it and understand our underlying emotional state. It's essential to become more of a private investigator, like Sherlock Holmes, and examine the evidence that is a part of our emotional case. Leaders who are more effective in mastering their emotions are also the most successful.

Now that we have a solid foundation on which to build our emotional awareness, it is time to deepen our understanding by taking things to the next level.

THE ROLE OF EFFECTIVE AND AFFECTIVE LABELING

Although many of us have not thought about labeling our emotions, a persuasive body of evidence supports its effectiveness.[23] However, despite its importance, research also shows us that this is no easy feat. Many of us struggle with how to accurately and fully label what we feel.

Affective labeling is the process by which we provide a more granular description of what we are experiencing. For example, rather than saying "I feel great," which is quite generic, use more specific labels such as *optimistic*, *energized*, or *excited*. The same works for negative emotions.

Effective labeling of our emotions is also important. Research strongly suggests that the more elaborate our description is about our emotional state, the better off we become. As one psychologist aptly described it, "We are constantly taking black and white photographs of the very colorful scenes of our lives."[24] The more detail we can provide to our life portrait, the richer and more meaningful the experience will be.

One of my all-time favorite studies was conducted at UCLA. Researchers recruited a group of eighty-eight volunteers who had an extreme phobia of spiders. What was especially interesting (and scary) about the experimental design was that each participant was expected to interact with a large tarantula—not the most pleasant experience for anyone, let alone for individuals with this intense phobia.

As part of the initial phase of the experiment, participants were divided into four groups. Although every individual would ultimately interact with the spider, each of the four groups was given separate instructions.

1. The first group was asked to label their emotional reactions to the experience as precisely as they could—the more words, the better. For example, they might say something like, "I'm anxious and frightened by the ugly, terrifying spider."

2. The second group was instructed to use less threatening or even minimizing language when describing their emotional state. Essentially, people were asked to talk about it as if they were not afraid. For example, "That spider can't hurt me. I'm much bigger than it is."

3. The third group was asked to share information unrelated to their experience. This was a distraction technique designed to divert attention away from their emotional state. An example might be, "I wonder what I should have for dinner tonight."

4. The fourth group was the control condition. They were asked not to say anything at all. They only interacted with the spider. Nothing more.

A week later, the study participants were brought back to interact with the same spider in an outdoor setting. The research team was keenly interested to see how the participants in each group responded to this repeat visit. The results were nothing short of extraordinary.

The researchers discovered that the group in which participants labeled their emotions performed significantly better than the other three groups in a couple of meaningful ways. First and foremost, these participants were in much closer proximity to the spider than their counterparts. They showed less hesitation, as indicated by their physical distance.

In addition, these individuals manifested significantly lower physiological responses to the encounter in that their palms were less sweaty than all the other participants. As noted by one of the lead scientists, "It's surprising that this minimal intervention action had a significant effect over exposure alone."[25]

Giving a more detailed voice to their experience helped them have a lower stress response. As explained by Matthew Lieberman, one of the study coauthors, "When spider-phobics say, 'I'm terrified of that nasty spider,' they're not learning something new; that's exactly what they were feeling—but now instead of just feeling it, they're saying it." [26]

The research also uncovered that the types and number of words the participants used had a significant effect on their outcomes. In particular, individuals who used a larger number of negative words performed better in terms of their willingness to get closer to the spider and experienced a less-intense physiological response. Describing their feelings more accurately enabled them to cope with the experience far better. The process of applying an honest label to their emotions helped reduce their anxiety and made it easier to cope.

These results are even more important when you think about the misperceptions we have about how we *should* deal with our emotions, especially negative ones. Lieberman states,

> We've published a series of studies where we asked people, "Which do you think would make you feel worse: looking at a disturbing image or looking at that disturbing image and choosing a negative emotional word to describe it?" Almost everyone said it would be worse to have to look at that image and focus on the negative by picking a negative word. People think that makes our negative emotions more intense. . . . Our intuitions here are wrong.[27]

Application to Leadership

This study can teach us several critical lessons in terms of how labeling our emotions benefits us.

First and foremost, the more precise we are acknowledging and labeling our emotions, the more effective we will be processing them. As we saw in the research study, participants who used more specific words to describe their anxiety reduced their subsequent stress response to a situation.

Another important benefit is that labeling our emotions better equips us to face our situations in a more constructive and productive way. Recall that the participants leaned into the experience and stood closer to the spider. They literally faced their fears. Before, they could not even fathom being in the same room as a spider, let alone taking steps to get closer to one. You can see how engaging in approach behaviors enables us to deal more effectively with whatever challenges we are navigating. Rather than run away, we face them head-on and take the appropriate action.

We can extend these core lessons in other areas of our emotional language to more effectively maneuver in our environment. For example, think about the possible application when comparing these two statements: "I feel lonely" versus "I feel awful."

The more generalized expression, "I feel awful," could be for a variety of reasons. Maybe I stayed up too late or ate too much. However, "I feel lonely" is highly specific. When you reflect on how you can more effectively address the situation based on both statements, "I feel lonely" provides a much clearer path forward than "I feel awful." By attaching the affective label of loneliness, we can identify practical solutions such as connecting with friends and family or finding other ways of reaching out. Better specificity brings a better pathway to resolution.

While we may sometimes use generalizations when it comes to managing our emotions, the more specific we are, the better equipped we become to deal with them.

LABELING OUR EMOTIONS

To improve our ability to label our emotions, this chart inspired by bestselling author, TED speaker, and highly regarded emotions expert Susan David is a powerful frame of reference.

A List of Emotions

Go beyond the obvious to identify exactly what you're feeling.

Angry	Sad	Anxious	Hurt	Embarrassed	Happy
Annoyed	Depressed	Afraid	Abandoned	Ashamed	Confident
Defensive	Disappointed	Bewildered	Aggrieved	Confused	Comfortable
Disgusted	Disillusioned	Cautious	Betrayed	Guilty	Content
Frustrated	Dismayed	Confused	Deprived	Inferior	Elated
Grumpy	Mournful	Nervous	Isolated	Isolated	Excited
Impatient	Paralyzed	Skeptical	Jealous	Lonely	Relaxed
Irritated	Pessimistic	Stressed	Shocked	Pathetic	Relieved
Offended	Regretful	Vulnerable	Tormented	Repugnant	Thankful
Spiteful	Tearful	Worried	Victimized	Self-conscious	Trusting

SEPARATING OUR FEELINGS
FROM OUR IDENTITIES

Although the specific wording we place on an emotion is clearly helpful, we need to be careful how we frame the experience. Consider the possible implications of describing our emotional state as "I *feel* lonely" versus "I *am* lonely." While you may initially feel this is a tedious exercise in wordsmithing (as these statements seem virtually identical), closer examination reveals they can trigger vastly different reactions.

Let's deal with these statements in reverse. Saying "I *am* lonely" is an identity statement. At its core, it's a reflection of *who I am*. When I say, "I am Craig Dowden, an executive coach and keynote speaker," this statement encapsulates my professional identity. When we invoke our identity with our words, it is more declarative and denotes a sense of permanence.

By contrast, saying "I *feel* lonely" is categorically different. Feelings are temporary. Unlike the statement above, this is not a reflection of who I am. Rather, it's simply an observation about how I feel *right now*, in this moment in time.

Being aware of how we label and describe emotions is impactful. When executives I work with start to incorporate this strategy into their day-to-day leadership, it assists them in handling their stress levels more effectively while having more influence with their teams.

HOW TO MANAGE OUR WORRIES

While everyone worries sometimes, we as leaders can often feel like the weight of the world is on our shoulders. It's a natural reaction because we have people counting on us to balance multiple, often competing, priorities.

Recent research suggests that we can invest, and ultimately waste, a tremendous amount of time and energy worrying. An intriguing study out of Pennsylvania State University involved participants with Generalized Anxiety Disorder who were asked to spend ten days writing in a Worry Outcome Journal.[28] Each time they started to worry about something, they logged it in their journal. They also answered questions about how likely they felt each worry would come to fruition and how anxious each worry made them feel. Over thirty days, the research team tracked their subsequent experiences.

Amazingly, 91.4% of their worries did not come true. In fact, the most common percentage of worries that ended up being untrue per person was 100%. Participants thought their fears would very likely come true, but in the vast majority of cases, they were wrong.

The other significant finding was that using a worry journal was highly beneficial; this practice resulted in significantly greater reductions in levels of worry after the intervention. The simple act of writing down their worries reduced the participants' anxiety. By writing them down, it became more obvious that their worries did not come to fruition.

Besides the Worry Outcome Journal, additional research suggests there's another powerful technique to manage our worries. It was developed by Dr. Thomas Borkovec, a psychology professor at Pennsylvania State University. His approach involved scheduling "worry time."

Back in 1981, Dr. Borkovec created "The Worry Group," which comprised fifteen psychologists and graduate students who had insomnia, primarily from worrying too much.[29] Instead of treating their insomnia, Dr. Borkovec proposed scheduling *Worry Time*, which involved setting aside a time and place every day to worry.

Every time a worry crept in, participants added it to their list of things to worry about. However, they could not worry about it until their allotted time. So if their *Worry Time* was scheduled for later that day, they had to put it aside until then.

Participants reported multiple benefits from scheduling *Worry Time*, including better quality sleep and spending less time worrying during the day. As a result of two experiments with this method, "At the end of four weeks, they reported on average spending 35 percent less time worrying than they had previously."

Here are some additional benefits of scheduling *Worry Time*:

▶ **Lower anxiety:** If we try to push worries out of our minds, they can keep creeping back in. When that happens, it gets in the way of our effectiveness. Scheduling *Worry Time* gives us confidence that we'll be taking care of that worry later on, which lowers our overall anxiety.

▶ **Maximize our productivity:** Our worries take up valuable cognitive and emotional real estate, making it tough to concentrate and perform at a high level. By writing our worries down and then returning to the task at hand, we minimize disruptions and maintain our focus. These are critical components of efficiency and effectiveness.

▶ **Allow the issue time and space to resolve itself:** By the time our *Worry Time* arrives, in many cases, things have shifted. The issue may have been resolved already or at least does not seem nearly as big an issue as it was when we scheduled time to worry about it.

What are the best techniques to use to create your own worry schedule? Dr. Borkovec's research gives some valuable answers:

▶ Create a thirty-minute *Worry Time* slot daily. Ideally, make it the same time and location each day.

▶ When worrisome thoughts come into your mind, write them down immediately. Then focus on something else such as finishing a task or moving around.

- ▶ Look at your list of worries only during your scheduled *Worry Time*.
- ▶ When it's your scheduled *Worry Time*, review your list and tackle one item at a time.
- ▶ If you run out of time, carry forward any unresolved items to the next day.

Scheduling time to worry and capturing our fears in a Worry Outcome Journal can equip us with powerful tools to manage the inevitable concerns that will arise as a leader.

TO VENT OR NOT TO VENT: THAT IS THE QUESTION!

Venting can give us a false sense of catharsis in the moment. Unfortunately, just like our emotions, it is contagious. When we engage in a venting session, the other person can follow our lead, trapping us in a cycle of co-rumination. We build on the other's negative emotions like a tennis match, hitting back and forth, which enhances our reactions and frustrations. By the time the conversation is over, both people are amped up with no resolution. Venting generally serves to manifest our anger rather than constructively address it.

Another downside of venting is that we tend to take on the role of the victim. We are exasperated about how powerless we feel in the situation. We are frustrated by our inability to change our circumstances. Not surprisingly, this sense of hopelessness inhibits our motivation to take action and can prolong our plight.

Despite these negative consequences, research suggests that not all venting is created equal. Finding someone who is highly skilled at listening and reframing our emotions can change the dynamic. While the content of a venting conversation may be the same, choosing wisely *who* we vent to can bring us to an entirely different outcome.

When we vent to someone who is highly skilled in reframing, the person who came in hot, feeling frustrated and angry, leaves more settled and equipped and with a different view of the situation. The next time you feel like you need a good venting session, prepare yourself for success by reflecting on these critical points:

- ▶ **Who should be my venting partner?** It is important to seek out individuals who we feel are good at reframing the situation. Think about the different people with whom you have vented. Did you feel better, the same, or worse after you left the conversation? If you felt better, chances are they are quite effective at reframing.

- ▶ **Be more mindful of the conversation.** Even if you select someone who is skilled at reframing, it is possible they can catch your emotions and turn the venting into a joint session. Be proactive by having your partner challenge your thinking/reactions by asking you, "How could you look at this differently?" "What might you be missing in this situation?" "What is another way you could think about this that could lower your frustration?" Using these types of questions facilitates our emotional processing and lowers our emotional temperature.

▶ **Resist the temptation to vent online.** While it may feel safer to vent online, evidence suggests the contagiousness of emotions may be even stronger in a virtual world.[30] If not for yourself, think about the impacts of your venting on others.

Mastering the skill of reframing greatly enhances our personal effectiveness and how our teams respond to our leadership. Another benefit is that we can play this role for our direct reports. We can deftly reframe their own frustrations when they come to us and empower them to focus their energy and attention on resolution rather than despair.

If you are unsure about how you can become better at reframing, think about the people on your list who you feel are experts in this domain. Sit down with them and share your admiration. Ask them directly about their thinking process. How do they listen to others? What types of questions do they find most effective?

Find exemplary models of this skill and seek them out as resources for your personal growth and development. It will serve you well.

THE POWER OF EMOTIONAL CONTAGION

Research shows that not only do we catch each other's emotions, but the more intense the emotion, the more "contagious" it becomes. Leaders need to be aware of this powerful effect because when we're in a collective environment, whether it's at work or with our family, the strongest emotion tends to dictate how everyone else around us feels. We need to ask ourselves, *Am I in an emotional state that I want other people to catch?*

Exposure to negative emotions exacts a cost. It impacts us psychologically, emotionally, and physiologically. Negative moods make a difference in how we make decisions and what we expect for outcomes. Like the case of worrying, our emotions alter how we view our possible futures. The *Annual Review of Psychology* also revealed the difference emotions can make in our judgment calls. If we are in a positive emotional state, we tend to make better judgments, but in a bad emotional state our judgments are more pessimistic.[31]

Here is an example of a client who lived the very real and detrimental effects of emotional contagion and learned how to counteract them.

EXECUTIVE COACHING CASE STUDY: TREATING EMOTIONAL CONTAGION

A client of mine, whom we'll call Michael, had achieved extraordinary results throughout his career. He had just been promoted from a senior VP position to take on a key C-suite role to drive revenue growth and innovation within the company.

I was brought in to work with him within the first twelve months of his appointment. Although he was delivering decent results, they were not quite at the level that people expected. There were also rumblings that he was starting to lose his team; a couple of members had already left the organization.

When I met with Michael, he was at a loss for what was happening. He had never experienced this before in his career. He was excited to challenge his team to produce the best ideas and felt he was a champion in this regard. Although people had shared ideas at the start of his tenure, no one had been speaking up lately. They sat and waited for him to provide some suggestions to debate. Even then, the energy was minimal at best, and people mostly just seemed to want to greenlight whatever was on the table.

To start our coaching work, I suggested to Michael that I conduct interviews with every member of his team to better understand his impact on the group. This was very revealing. While everyone acknowledged that Michael was highly talented and exceptionally bright, his style was bringing people down. In brainstorming sessions, he would always start with what was wrong with any idea presented. Oftentimes he wouldn't let the person finish their thought. He would interrupt and railroad their suggestions.

Michael also had a terrible habit of sighing loudly once someone finished their pitch. He routinely rolled his eyes or exhibited other signs of disinterest. This toxic combination created a culture in which people quickly learned to stay quiet and wait for Michael to "tell us the right answer." This was the safest and most efficient thing to do, even though everyone was frustrated by it. They all recognized it was harming the performance of the team, but they felt it was the best strategy.

Michael was shocked when he heard their reactions. He thought he was creating an environment where people could thrive. He relished the role of challenger because he thought he could spark the best in his people, not the worst.

I coached Michael to use more open-ended questions with his team. When someone suggested something he thought was off base, rather than dismissing it outright, he would prompt them with "Tell me more." When he thought about saying something negative or critical, we worked on developing more open-ended questions. For example, rather than saying, "This will never work," I coached him to start asking, "How do you see this fitting into our time line for this client?"

The feedback was immediate and very positive. His team noticed the changes in his behavior. Better yet, the meetings were much more energized and animated. The quality of ideas and team results quickly improved. They launched more ambitious ideas than ever before. Accountability went up as people felt more a part of the proposed solutions. Michael learned an invaluable lesson in the power of emotional contagion.

CEO MASTERCLASS WITH ALAN MULALLY: ON MASTERING OUR EMOTIONS

Throughout his career, Alan has recognized the power and importance of emotions. For instance, when considering moving from Boeing to Ford, he emphasized that his feelings played a pivotal role in his decision-making process.

"When people ask me for advice about how to make the best quality decisions, I tell them not to just focus on *what* you're thinking about the situation, but also focus on *how* you're feeling. Otherwise, you will miss important information."

While our emotions are invaluable data points, they must be managed properly. This is where the "Working Together" Management System keeps things in check. A perfect illustration of this happened early on at Ford during a Business Plan Review (BPR).

At the first BPRs, Alan witnessed a powerful example of how the "Working Together" principles and practices created a safe environment and culture of transparency early in his tenure with Ford. "I remember the first time the leadership team was trying to decide whether they were going to trust me on color coding. We had over three hundred charts from teams all around the world. At the time, we were projected to lose $17 billion that year, but *all* the color charts were green."

When he asked the team if anything might not be going well given they were forecast to lose $17 billion, all eyes went to the floor. "Nobody wanted to look up." In that moment, Alan realized there was a strong culture of fear.

Undaunted, Alan stayed committed to "Working Together" and the BPR process. Eventually, one of his senior executives included a red indicator. Although it was the right thing to do, the executive's colleagues felt it was the end of his career—and even wished him well before the meeting.

Upon seeing the red status, Alan stood up and clapped his hands. The people in the room who thought the executive would be punished or, worse, fired, were surprised when Alan instead said, "Thank you. This is great visibility." Then he turned to the rest of the team and asked, "Any thoughts on how we can help?" After getting over their initial shock, several members of the team jumped in, offering to provide experts from their areas or share their experiences.

The transition to getting more yellows and reds on the board didn't happen overnight. But it did happen. Alan made another smart move to manage emotions and enforce a culture of safety over fear.

He recalls, "I invited the executive to sit next to me at the next meeting. People realized that rather than being punished, this executive was being rewarded for his transparency. Over the next several meetings, the charts went from all green to a rainbow of reds, yellows, and greens."

Another brilliant way Alan addressed the potential impact of managing secrets was by calling the red status items "gems" instead of problems, the reason being that "the reds represent mission-critical issues. It is essential that they come to the surface, or they can capsize your business."

Alan summarizes the power of "Working Together" in this way: "If you don't have an environment where people feel comfortable and safe to share what's really going on, you're not going to be able to work together to bring the One Plan to life."

CONCLUDING THOUGHTS

Despite the popularity of the expression, "It's not personal, it's just business," nothing could be further from the truth. Every aspect of our professional lives is personal, and this is routinely expressed through our emotions. If these are left unchecked, we can allow the darker angels of our nature to drive our behavior. However, this common destination is not necessarily our destiny.

Embracing the importance of becoming an emotional detective and understanding what these data points are trying to tell us is foundational for us to be at our best. We must spend time recognizing our triggers and our counterstrategies. Only then can we maximize our potential and keep ourselves, our teams, and our organizations focused on the path forward.

CHAPTER 3

MASTERING OUR RESILIENCE

*It's your reaction to adversity, not adversity itself that
determines how your life's story will develop.*
—Dieter F. Uchtdorf

Building resilience in leaders and organizations is
widely viewed as mission critical. The speed of
change is intense, so we must be prepared to adapt.
We cannot afford to hold on to the frames of yesterday
to tackle the challenges and opportunities of tomorrow.
We must dream bigger and be prepared to push
ourselves further. We will encounter unanticipated yet
critical challenges. Mastering our resilience is at the
heart of continuing our pursuit of individual, team, and
organizational excellence.

AN INTRODUCTION TO RESILIENCE AND STRESS

Before exploring how we can enhance our resilience, it is important to answer a couple of foundational questions.

What Is Resilience?

Resilience represents our ability to bounce back from challenging events. How long does it take for us to return to baseline after we've encountered a setback or difficulty? The time it takes us to recover is important. If I bounce back quickly, that means I am more capable of dealing with the different demands I'm facing. The faster I can return to normal, the faster I can move forward.

Can Resilience Be Learned?

Another question that comes up frequently in my workshops is whether our level of resilience is determined by nature or nurture. While many people believe nurture is the driving force, I'll admit it is a bit of a trick question. We come into life with a biological set point around our propensity to be resilient.[32] The best news for every one of us is that we have the capacity to grow our level of resilience. The trick is that, just like any other skill, we need to engage in dedicated, focused practice.

For example, if I want to enhance my level of cardiovascular fitness, I need to go on long walks. I have to get on my exercise bike or go for a run. I will not improve my cardio without doing something about it. The same holds true if I want to build more lean muscle mass. I must hit the weights and do the necessary reps so I can reap the rewards. The process of building our resilience muscle is identical: we must exercise for it to grow.

What Causes Us to Feel Stress?

Across the countless studies that have examined this question, a primary cause of stress is a perceived lack of control. This happens when I feel that no matter what I say or do, my circumstances will not change. When I feel like I cannot influence my environment, my stress response skyrockets. This is one of the reasons why leading experts recommend that we focus on things that are within our control and let go of those that are not.

One of the most powerful studies I have come across invited volunteers to solve a series of complex problems. Participants were instructed to wear head-phones that played loud, annoying music while they completed the task. Not surprisingly, their performance was significantly worse when compared to the partici-pants who heard no music.

However, another group was exposed to the same loud, obnoxious music, but in this case they were told they could turn it off if they wanted. Recall that these problems were quite complex in nature and required as much attention as possible. This simple shift in perceived control resulted in their performance improving to the level of those who were played no music at all.

But here's the fascinating part: *virtually no one turned off the music*. The fact that they knew they *could* turn off the music as soon as it became too much was sufficient for them to be able to divert their energy and attention to the task at hand. Nothing changed other than the knowledge that they could alter their environment if they chose to do so.

What Is the Difference Between Pressure and Stress?

One of the most transformative ideas I have come across was developed by the Center for Creative Leadership (CCL), which highlighted the difference between pressure and stress. According to CCL, *pressure* represents the extent of the demands that our external environment places on us. *Stress*, however, is our internal belief about our ability to manage those demands.

This distinction illustrates why two people who seem identical can have entirely different stress responses to the same situation. In one case, an individual—let's call her Sara—feels completely capable of managing the pressure. She survives and even thrives in the situation. Paul, however, cracks under the pressure because he does not feel capable of handling it.

There are a couple of crucial takeaways here. We can infer that pressure is external and stress is internal. While many people believe that stress happens to us, it is our interpretation of the situation that leads to the emotion. Being aware that we have the power to influence our stress response is critical to building resilience.

This distinction provides us with the key to a thriving future. Specifically, the difference between Sara and Paul lies in their confidence to deal with their situation. Research also shows that those of us who take a more resource-based approach to our situations engage in more adaptive coping. By gathering the support we need, we increase our confidence in our ability to manage the pressure we are under.

When we feel under-resourced, mastering our resilience involves identifying pathways to change our trajectory. We can and should ask ourselves empowering questions such as, *What resources can I access to feel more confident in my ability to deal with these demands? Who can offer me support or relevant insight?* Focusing on proactive steps we can take brings us to a position of strength and agency rather than one of weakness and victimhood.

EXECUTIVE COACHING CASE STUDY: FOSTERING A RESILIENT CULTURE

The pace of change continues to escalate in our society and organizations. No matter where we live and work, we are affected by it. One of my clients, Allison, was in a high-growth, leading technology industry. She was accustomed to driving innovative solutions to emerging problems.

Unfortunately, recent events had put even more downward pressure on her team. With increasingly aggressive demands from their customers and management, it felt like they were sometimes drinking out of a fire hose.

The performance of the team had dropped over the past several months. So I conducted a 360-feedback interview process to better understand what was happening.

People very quickly pointed out that while there was no doubt they were a high-potential team, they had developed a bad habit of imagining the worst-case scenarios. When a request was made, people, usually starting with Allison, would openly complain. When something new was placed on her desk, she would show up to team meetings and say in an exasperated tone, "How can we possibly add this to our to-do list?"

Allison didn't realize that her reactions derailed the project before it even began. By openly questioning whether they could even accomplish it, people disconnected early and were quite disgruntled. The team agreed they lost the ability to thrive under pressure.

When I spoke with Allison about pressure and stress and the benefits of taking a resource-based approach, she was very interested to learn more. She recognized what she was doing wasn't working and likely made matters worse.

We developed a list of questions she could ask herself and her team members (one-on-one and in a group) about how they could tackle their workload. Here are a few examples:

▶ What resources do we need from one another or the organization to tackle this challenge?

▶ What are our biggest areas of concern about this project? In what area(s) are we most comfortable?

▶ How can each of us best support our team in the execution of this project?

▶ What barriers do we foresee getting in the way of us being at our best?

These questions paid immediate dividends during their next team meeting. When answering the first question, the team took a more systematic approach and broke down the project into concrete steps with associated time lines. This fine-tuned perspective led to the realization that they would need an additional resource. Armed with this knowledge, Allison approached the CEO to secure support.

A new employee who had joined another division was assigned to assist in the project as a way to get to know other areas of the organization and build strategic relationships. The team was thrilled with this transfer and felt more empowered to proceed.

In debriefing their experience, team members shared that in the past, they would have spent a lot of time complaining about the situation, both in the meeting and beyond. This wasted a lot of precious time and energy they could have dedicated to working on the project.

Also, the team would have just plowed ahead and taken it all on themselves, not pausing to ask themselves strategic questions about what could make things easier. As time went on, even though they did not always receive what they asked (even in the case of the new hire, they were hoping for a more experienced employee), the very act of identifying the required resources empowered them to tackle their challenges with more enthusiasm and effectiveness.

MANAGING OUR STRESS MINDSET

While the research of Carol Dweck on growth and fixed mindsets has revolutionized our understanding and appreciation of the impacts of our mindsets, extraordinary work is also being done relating to how our mindset affects our experience of stress and resilience.

To start, I would like you to think about the extent to which you agree or disagree with the following statements (strongly disagree, disagree, neutral, agree, strongly agree):

▶ Stress is harmful
▶ Stress is natural
▶ Stress is beneficial

Remember your answers.

When I ask these questions to a live or virtual audience, the results are consistent. Most people agree with the statement "Stress is harmful." The question that generally receives the lowest score is "Stress is beneficial"; people are either neutral or disagree with this position. While your answers may mirror the preceding ones, evidence suggests our beliefs may be much more important than you think. Let me explain.

In her insightful bestseller *The Upside of Stress*, Kelly McGonigal presents a compelling study that involved over thirty thousand people to examine the relationship between someone's stress level and their risk of early mortality.

The initial conclusion will likely not surprise you: higher levels of stress were associated with a higher risk of early mortality. Here's where things get interesting. The research team went a level deeper.

In particular, they were curious about the mindsets that people possessed about stress, similar to my brief survey above. The results show that the mindset of the individual plays a significant role in the outcomes. In fact, the only group in which the relationship between higher stress and early mortality risk exists is when people *believe* that stress is harmful. For people who did not possess this belief, there is zero relationship.

Another interesting insight emerged. People who held the opposite view (e.g., stress is natural or beneficial) have the lowest risk of early mortality, even compared to those who report lower levels of stress in their lives yet hold the belief that stress is harmful.

Think about that for a moment: my belief about whether stress is harmful to me directly and significantly impacts my chances of dying early. This is an extraordinarily powerful example of why we must pay attention to our mindset.

One powerful and practical takeaway is to ask yourself what your mindset about stress is and how it affects your experience on a psychological, emotional, and physical level. Remember, these mindsets not only impact the experience of stress but also have deadly consequences.

Creating a (Resilience) Mantra

There is considerable evidence that mantras (silent or vocal repetition of a key phrase) have powerful benefits for our psychological and emotional well-being. While mantras are typically associated with meditation or yoga, one recent study discovered that mantras can be just as effective for people who do not regularly engage in meditation.[33]

Researchers revealed that individuals who repeated a mantra created a significant shift in their neural activity. Specifically, activity in the brain region responsible for internal evaluation, rumination, and mind-wandering improved. When compared to a control group in a resting state, participants who employed a mantra achieved an elevated state of psychological well-being. This demonstrates the power of mantras to bolster our resilience and stress management.

While I encourage you to create your own mantras, here are a few examples to get you started:

- My mistakes are valuable teachers. Learn from them.
- I am not afraid of a challenge. Bring it on!
- Being my best is about testing my limits.
- I'm going to figure a way out of this. The important thing is not to give up.
- If this were easy, everybody would be doing it.

REFRAMING OUR STRESS MINDSET

One helpful strategy to refashion our relationship with stress is to think about it from multiple perspectives. When I'm delivering a workshop on the topic, I ask people how stress may be helpful to them.

While many answers are provided, one of the most common is that stress provides us with activation energy. We are primed to take action on whatever we are facing. We are mobilized and inspired to tackle our challenges. This is one of the many ways that stress can benefit us.

People also mention that we tend to reach out to people in our support networks when we are feeling down. We connect with our loved ones, lean into our friendships, or ask our colleagues for help. These actions provide us with the emotional support we need to navigate these challenges.

I encourage you to write down a list of positives that stress brings to your life. What are the ways in which stress enhances your existence? What would you miss in life without it?

Kelly McGonigal also provides a powerful three-step process we can use to channel our stress more constructively.[34] Here is how it works:

First, McGonigal suggests you acknowledge your stress. We must acknowledge that we are experiencing stress, or else it can create various challenges for us. When we fail to acknowledge stress, we are more inclined to avoid it or pretend it doesn't exist.

Fundamentally, stress is our mind, our body, or our heart telling us that we need to pay attention to something. By avoiding it, we engage in maladaptive coping behaviors such as binge drinking or procrastination. Unfortunately, this is highly ineffective because we are not dealing with the root problem, which leads to it getting worse.

Think of some of the top advice given in fields such as medicine or conflict management. What do the experts say? Address an issue as soon as possible. Don't let an infection fester, whether it's in our body or in our relationships. If we do, the consequences will be harsher, more complicated, and harder to undo. The larger the issue becomes, the less motivated we are to confront it.

Second, McGonigal recommends demonstrating acceptance. Stress generally comes from something we care about. Recognize that these feelings are coming from a place of importance. Accept the source of caring.

Third, channel the energy in a positive way. Stress is an evolutionary response to mobilize us for action. When we feel stressed, we are activated. Rather than let that energy go to waste, we can choose to deploy it toward the issue at hand. Ultimately, we have an opportunity to commit to using the energy in a positive way.

I'll share a personal example. I deliver a lot of keynote speeches, both virtually and in person. Every time I am about to speak to an audience, I start to feel stress, no matter how many times I have delivered that talk before. So the first thing I do is acknowledge that stress.

I also accept my feelings of stress. I remind myself that it's a natural response to my situation because I care about my audience. They have invested money and/or time to hear me speak. I want to make sure they get the maximum return on their investment and that I exceed their expectations. I remind myself that all good public speaking is born of nerves!

Now that I have acknowledged and accepted my feelings of stress, I am empowered to choose how to use that activation energy. I can decide to show up with as much enthusiasm as possible. I can provide as many resources and activities as I have available. I can provide my contact information for follow-up. I can focus on countless ways to bring my best to this experience.

CEO MASTERCLASS WITH ALAN MULALLY ON MASTERING OUR RESILIENCE

Although each of the leadership qualities within this book integrates beautifully with the "Working Together" Management System, mastering our resilience is an exceptional example.

Recall that stress occurs when we feel we do not have the necessary resources at our disposal to tackle the pressures we face. The very label "Working Together" indicates that we have access to people who can assist us in countless ways—for example, by providing us with "extra bodies" to power through our deliverables when we are over capacity, providing ideas or expertise that can help us identify solutions to our greatest challenges, and providing emotional support that can motivate us to continue with the confidence that we have supporters when we need them.

As Alan explains, "We know we are going to run into unanticipated issues and setbacks because this is an innovative creative process. We expect the unexpected and we expect to deal with it by "Working Together." By "Working Together," we are never alone. We all trust the process to help each other."

Resilience cascades into the color-coded check-ins as well. Reds are classified as "gems" because they represent opportunities for positive intervention. They represent a challenge to be solved together as opposed to something that should be avoided or feared. We can draw on the individual and collective intelligence in the room to decide what our best course of action is to overcome our predicament.

There are other ways that the color-coding system fosters resilience from people who are "Working Together." As Alan highlights, "When one of your elements is red, it doesn't mean that *you're* a red. It means that *the situation you are in is red*. This is a critical distinction."

Although this may seem subtle, it is a brilliant and powerful difference. Resilience comes from the confidence that we can handle the pressures we face. If "reds" were perceived as a reflection of an individual versus situational quality, this likely could and would significantly impact the level of confidence, ultimately undermining resilience. It would likely lead to a focus on *What is wrong with* me? versus *What is wrong with the* situation? It shifts from asking, *Why can't I figure this out?* to, *Who can help me figure this out?*

Since it is expected that everyone may have all three colors within their status reports, nobody feels like they are a failure for reporting them. In fact, it would be odd if you did not have a red from time to time. This level of transparency is celebrated for providing outstanding visibility. Alan reinforced that idea perfectly when he applauded the executive who showed the first red at Ford and thanked him for the great visibility.

Evidence suggests that one of the most scientifically supported ways to increase our resilience is to remember times in the past when we have successfully overcome adversity. The reasoning is that if we have done it before, we can do it again!

"Working Together" provides continuous examples of this. This culture and system is resilient. When we move our status updates from red to yellow to green, we appreciate that "Working Together" works. Even if we forget this fact, those around us can be a powerful and positive reminder. "When we trust the process and each other, we can accomplish and overcome anything and develop a better plan."

As we discussed in chapter 1, ambiguity is a potent predictor of anxiety and stress. When things are unclear, we can create worst-case scenarios. Our worries can get the better of us, and we can panic and make poor decisions as a result of our fears.[35] Once again, "Working Together" provides immediate visibility into the issues and a plan for all of us to turn the reds to yellows to greens.

As we are continually basing our discussions on facts and data, it minimizes the chances that either the situation or our emotional response will get blown out of proportion. The BPR meetings keep us grounded in reality.

"The most important thing is to deal with reality. Not the way you want it to be, or you hoped it would be. When you're building airplanes and making cars, you have to know what the reality is. If you don't know the reds and yellows, you can't turn them to greens. The same goes with the rest of the aspects of the business."

Many people think that nobody feels the heat like the CEO, who is ultimately responsible for the results of their organization. This weight is more pronounced when you are leading a publicly traded company. When you occupy the corner office of a global, highly scrutinized brand, the weight may feel overwhelming. Since Alan did this not once but twice, you would think he would be at the greatest risk of having a few sleepless nights.

"People asked me all the time how I could sleep at night," Alan remembers. "My answer was simple. I slept really well because we, the entire team, have had a Business Plan Review meeting every week. We all know all the greens, yellows, and reds. We know everything that's going on and so do all the stake-holders. We are always working on the areas that need special attention. The best thing we each can do as leaders is to get some sleep and come back with our "Working Together" positive, can-do, find-a-way attitude and skills."

CONCLUDING THOUGHTS

Our relationship with stress plays a significant role in our ability to be resilient. We each can face the same pressure in the same situation, but whether we feel stress is greatly influenced by how we view our circumstances. Recognizing the key role that we play in creating our own stress response is vital for leaders to understand.

Awareness alone is not enough. We must take the learning from our experiences and recognize the steps we need to take when the pressure builds. It is critical to be aware of our stress mindset so we can transform it to one of flourishing. This acts as a powerful buffer against those potentially negative forces and allows us and the people around us to be champions, rather than victims, of adversity.

CHAPTER 4

MASTERING OUR STRENGTHS

The purpose of life is to discover your gift.
The work of life is to develop it.
The meaning of life is to give your gift away.
—DAVID VISCOTT

Research tells us that people who use their strengths more often are significantly more resilient, engaged, and successful than their counterparts. Although evidence strongly suggests that we benefit from capitalizing on our strengths, what exactly does this mean in practice? How do we know what our strengths are? How do we identify them? How can we leverage them for our maximum advantage?

This chapter provides answers to each of these critical questions. We will explore what strengths mean to you as a leader and as a human being. We will also examine how to identify your strengths, why it matters, and the purpose they serve. Bringing all of this together, we will tap into how to leverage our strengths for the greater good and maximize their potential.

THE SCIENCE OF STRENGTHS

Before we begin examining our strengths, we need to clarify what the term means. According to the Gallup organization, strengths represent the "ability to consistently provide near-perfect performance in a specific activity."[36]

An often overlooked yet important element of the Gallup definition relates to the relationship between talents and strengths. In their view, everyone is born with innate talents that have the capacity to become strengths. However, this happens only when we dedicate the time and energy into appropriately developing our talents.

This is a perfect illustration of the expression "wasting our talent." Regardless of how much natural ability we may possess, if we do not invest in this potential, we fail to reap the rewards. If we leave our talents untapped, they do not turn into strengths.

Now that we have a fundamental understanding of what strengths look like, an equally important question relates to how they impact our effectiveness as leaders. Research conducted by Zenger Folkman, a leading authority on 360-degree feedback, illuminates the answer. Based on their data, when leaders showed no strengths, they were rated in the 34th percentile of leadership effectiveness. However, their average effectiveness virtually doubled (up to 64 percent) by introducing a single strength.

Their results also show that each additional strength provides a gain of 8–9 percent in overall effectiveness, up to a maximum of five strengths. At this point, we are in the 95th percentile of performance and the effectiveness scores level off, no matter how many additional strengths we develop.

BEWARE OUR FATAL FLAWS

Given this research, a common question emerges: "Should we always focus on strengths?" While the answer to this question is predominantly *yes*, there is one exception: when we have a fatal flaw.

A powerful way to visualize this idea is to imagine we are at a dock and about to board our sailboat to travel to a neighboring island. We need to reach our destination before nightfall, which is a little over an hour away. We have a little bit of time to spare but should set out in the next ten to fifteen minutes at most.

During our safety check, our sails are in great condition and there is a strong tailwind, which will be helpful for our journey. Looking good so far. However, as we are about to cast off, we notice a small hole on the port side. It is well above water level and near the railing. It appears water will come in only if there happens to be a large wave, perhaps created by a nearby Jet Ski. However, the chances of that happening appear to be slim.

Should you delay your departure to focus on that hole or just get on your way to make it to your destination before dark?

Unless you have had a very bad experience or perhaps have a strong fear of water, I imagine you would say this is not a big deal. We can repair the small hole if needed the following morning after we arrive. It is much better to proceed rather than risk being stranded overnight.

In this example, the sails represent our strengths. They provide us with maximum momentum. The quality of our sails primarily dictates our ability to get to our destination. The hole, conversely, represents our weaknesses. Now, you can imagine an even larger hole, but if it's near the handrails, it really does not pose a threat.

Using this analogy, you can see why it is in our best interest to carry on—with one exception. Let's say the hole is quite large and we're taking on a lot of water. At this point, it does not matter how much effort we put into rigging the sails. The boat is not going to move very fast, and the longer we leave it, the more we put ourselves in danger. When this happens, we need to correct this fatal flaw before setting sail.

Zenger Folkman provided compelling evidence supporting the importance of addressing our fatal flaws.[37] Based on a database of more than six thousand leaders, they divided leaders into three categories:

1. Possessing a fatal flaw with no strengths
2. No fatal flaws and no strengths
3. No fatal flaws with profound strengths

On average, the leaders who possessed a fatal flaw without any strengths operated at the 18th percentile of effectiveness. When the leaders did not have any fatal flaws and no strengths, their effectiveness jumped to about 50 percent. Last but not least, when leaders exhibited profound strengths without fatal flaws, their performance spiked to 81 percent.

The evidence is abundantly clear that eliminating fatal flaws is mission critical during our time to lead.

BARRIERS TO USING OUR STRENGTHS

Another common question I am asked is, "If strengths are so great, why don't we use them more often?"

One of the primary barriers is evolutionary in nature. We are conditioned to look out for danger. From the earliest days of human history, we were constantly scanning our environment for threats. Where could things go wrong? Or the question put even more simply, "What could kill us or cause us significant harm?"

A considerable amount of research shows that we are strongly biased toward the negative. It is built into our DNA. *The Review of General Psychology* published an article in 2001 titled "Bad Is Stronger than Good," which summarized decades of social science research and explained how this "danger mentality" still affects us today.[38]

Looking for potential problems can lead us away from focusing on our strengths. "Survival requires urgent attention to possible bad outcomes, but it is less urgent with regard to good ones." The allure of this type of thinking is that the "problem" feels more urgent, more important. Our attention is focused on the negative because of our primal need to avoid danger.

Think about our education system. When a child comes home with a report card that includes several As and a C, where do parents focus their attention? While they may applaud the As, the bulk of the discussion is likely dedicated to the C. The mentality is that we need to fix that C as soon as possible. The same thing happens when we transition into a work environment.

During many, if not most, professional development conversations, the leader primarily focuses on gaps or "areas of opportunity." Although positive results may be referenced in passing, development areas are examined under a powerful magnifying glass.

While an action plan sounds great in principle, in reality it often focuses exclusively on our weaknesses, even when they are small holes in our ship. A powerful, strategic question becomes, "What would happen if we paid more attention to our strengths?"

Zenger Folkman decided to look more closely into the answer.[39] They divided a group of leaders who were developing an improvement plan into two categories. The first group solely looked at their weaknesses, while the second incorporated both strengths and weaknesses into their plan.

The group who focused solely on their weaknesses showed a 12 percent improvement in performance. You may be thinking, *That's not bad. Why is Craig so down on this? It works.* Here's why. The group who included their strengths and weaknesses in their development plan had three times better performance than the group that focused only on weaknesses (which represents a 36 percent improvement). This makes a compelling case as to the importance of ensuring we do not forget about strengths when we are looking at getting the best out of ourselves. In fact, it may be the most important thing we do for ourselves as individuals as well as for how we choose to lead our teams and organizations.

Another barrier getting in the way of using our strengths is that we often have no idea what they are. Sometimes we can think we have strengths in areas where we don't. In other cases, we don't even know where to begin. We haven't even thought about the question. Our level of awareness when it comes to our strengths is sorely lacking.

Even more concerning, if we do not know what our strengths are, how can we possibly leverage them? How can we find new ways to put them into practice to help us become better human beings and better leaders? This lack of self-knowledge is a barrier in and of itself.

IDENTIFYING OUR STRENGTHS

Although numerous strengths assessments are available for purchase on the market, a free, evidence-based, online strengths assessment is available from the VIA Institute of Character.[40] This tool has been administered to well over twelve million people and provides a robust analysis of your strengths.

Each report provides the rank order of twenty-four character strengths, which are subsumed under six virtues. Special emphasis is placed on your top five. If you so choose, you can pay a premium to unlock even more actionable insight.

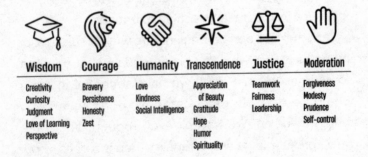

Wisdom	Courage	Humanity	Transcendence	Justice	Moderation
Creativity	Bravery	Love	Appreciation of Beauty	Teamwork	Forgiveness
Curiosity	Persistence	Kindness	Gratitude	Fairness	Modesty
Judgment	Honesty	Social Intelligence	Hope	Leadership	Prudence
Love of Learning	Zest		Humor		Self-control
Perspective			Spirituality		

Leveraging Our Strengths

When I completed the VIA assessment, my strengths showed up as follows:

1. **Leadership:** I mobilize groups and bring them together to function at a high level, often in the role of the leader.

2. **Judgment:** I carefully examine issues from multiple angles, taking a balanced perspective to situations and avoiding jumping to conclusions.

3. **Social Intelligence:** I am aware of the emotional dynamics at play, both individually and collectively. I understand what people need from me and from one another to support a common goal.

4. **Zest:** I have a high degree of positive energy and enthusiasm. I do not do things half-heartedly. I show up ready to go.

5. **Hope:** I possess an optimistic view of the future. I tend to see opportunities rather than obstacles. I believe anything is possible if I approach a situation with the appropriate level of focus. I may not get all the way there, but I will be closer than if I did nothing.

You can see how my profile fits very well for my role as an executive coach and keynote speaker on leadership, team, and organizational excellence. However, a key element of a strengths-based approach is to look for ways to leverage them as much as possible. To examine how we can do this, here is a three-step process I routinely use with my clients.

Step One: Identify Your Strengths

List your five signature strengths on a sheet of paper. Here are mine to give you an example.

1. Leadership
2. Judgment
3. Social intelligence
4. Zest
5. Hope

Step Two: Strengths-Usage (Current State)

Create a scorecard to track how well you leverage each of your strengths in your current role using the following scale: 0 = you are not using that strength at all; 10 = you are using it perfectly. Remember, be honest with yourself. The purpose of this exercise is not to inflate the results.

Signature Strength	How well do I leverage your strengths in my current role?
1. Leadership	
2. Judgment	
3. Social intelligence	
4. Zest	
5. Hope	

Step Three: Strengths-Usage (Future State)

Once you have scored yourself using the preceding scorecard, ask yourself the next question: *what opportunities exist to use my strengths more often?*

Don't limit yourself to only considering how you can create more opportunities to engage in your current strengths-related activities. Think outside the box and reflect on new ways to do this. If you're stuck, ask your colleagues or trusted mentors.

The final question in the set asks you to consider who can support you to use your strengths more often. Could you enlist the support of your supervisor? Could you ask a colleague? Should you share your aspirations with your romantic partner or best friend to hold you accountable? By building a community of support, you maximize the chances you will be successful.

If you want to take this exercise to the next level, apply the same three questions to other domains of your life, like with your family or friends.

Don't stop there. Use this powerful exercise when engaged in one-on-one conversations with your direct reports. I am including the following table to provide an example of how to do this.

Signature Strength	What opportunities exist to use your strengths more often in your current role?	Who can support you in using your strengths more often?
1. Leadership		
2. Judgment		
3. Social intelligence		
4. Zest		
5. Hope		

BUILDING RESILIENCE THROUGH STRENGTHS

Although the previous chapter discussed the importance of resilience, one of the most empirically supported resilience-building exercises incorporates the concept of strengths.

Here's how it works. Think of a challenging situation in the past that you felt was impossible to overcome. It could have been three weeks, three months, or even three years ago. After you have identified this situation, ask yourself three questions:

1. What strengths did you draw on to successfully overcome it?
2. What resources did you access to successfully overcome it?
3. What did you learn about yourself?

The structure of these questions is quite powerful. In answering the first question, you are drawing your attention to internal resources—your strengths—that support you and are especially important during times of extreme challenge. By drawing attention to your strengths, you can think about the extent to which they apply to your current situation. If they don't, what other strengths do you possess that could also be relevant?

The second question focuses on your external resources. For example, did you take a course or watch a webinar? Read a book? Speak with a mentor, colleague, or family member? Just as you did with the first question, examine whether these same sources of support are relevant to your current predicament. If not, can you follow the same process you used so effectively last time?

The last question is also very important. The key lesson you learned is that you have what it takes to overcome exceptional adversity. Remember the setup to this exercise: think about a time when you were facing a situation you felt was impossible and that you successfully overcame. If you faced a so-called impossible situation before and lived to tell the tale, why not now?

EXECUTIVE COACHING CASE STUDY: TAKING A STRENGTHS-BASED APPROACH WITH YOUR TEAM

Without question, Charlie was a top-performing CEO. His organization had won multiple awards for culture, and their financial results were consistently exceeding expectations.

When the pandemic hit, his organization was impacted. Their supply chain was disrupted and other changes they were in the process of making were delayed. This led to some challenging times.

During one of our coaching sessions, Charlie asked about different approaches he could take to re-engage his team. I asked if he had considered a strengths-based approach. He mentioned he had heard of the concept before but thought it was more pop psychology than rigorous leadership practice.

After briefly reviewing the evidence, Charlie was intrigued and decided to give it a go. He took the VIA Strengths Assessment and really enjoyed our debrief of his results. He was convinced to have his team complete the assessment as well.

He informed his team that his intention was for everyone to share their results openly and talk about how they could best leverage their individual and collective strengths profile in their work. While some were a little hesitant and even skeptical, they decided to try it.

Charlie opened their next meeting by asking his team to guess his profile. He was surprised to learn they were more accurate than he was. They openly discussed how his strengths contributed to the performance of the team and how some of his lesser strengths may be creating a few challenges. Interestingly, Charlie rated his lesser strengths higher, which he realized may have been contributing to the difficulties his team was experiencing.

As people spoke in turn around the virtual table, Charlie noticed a palpable energy. People laughed and said, "I knew it!" as everyone took turns sharing what made them great.

According to Charlie, the benefits didn't stop there. The discussion continued long after the initial meeting. Team members started assigning tasks based on their strengths profile and provided one another with advice on how their individual strengths might serve a particular project. It also gave everyone a common language for discussion. Better still, people enjoyed talking about what was right about themselves and their team.

Their engagement and performance improved very quickly. As the economy turned and their delayed initiatives were completed, results outpaced expectations. When they hired for a new role, team members suggested to Charlie that he use their collective strengths profile as an important criterion for selection. When the new hire joined, she possessed the key strength the team felt they were missing. They have not looked back since.

CEO MASTERCLASS WITH ALAN MULALLY: ON MASTERING OUR STRENGTHS

Alan has integrated a strengths-based philosophy throughout his "Working Together" Management System. In particular, mastering our strengths fully informs the approach to both project and people management.

"When you are 'Working Together,'" Alan says, "you focus on the positive. It is not that you ignore the negative. It's about deciding where you're going to spend most of your time. We choose to look for what's possible and how we can get there."

This is wonderfully illustrated within the context of the BPR. Red status updates represent areas where things are off plan and the team has no idea how to address the gap. When this happens, everyone quickly mobilizes to think about how they can best respond to the situation. The questions they consider are highly strengths-focused.

As Alan advises, "When we are 'Working Together,' we ask questions such as, 'What talents or skills do we need to address this most effectively? Who is in the best position to help? We consider our individual and collective strengths to move things forward.'"

This intentional focus on strengths allows the most qualified people in the room to assist. Egos or position are not part of the equation. Talent is the deciding factor, which maximizes efficiency and effectiveness.

When it comes to people management and executive development in particular, a strengths-based approach is front and center. As Alan explains, "I never think of weaknesses. Everyone has talents. Our ultimate goal is to continually leverage and develop our individual and collective talents so we can thrive while 'Working Together.'"

This is manifested in numerous ways. First, executive development plans are about enhancing strengths. As Alan says, "We do not settle for the status quo. Even when someone has immense talent, there are always opportunities to grow. We search for new and creative ways to leverage the talents in our team. That is at the heart of 'Working Together.'"

The positive effects of this practice are bolstered by each executive sharing their development plans with one another. By doing this, everyone can receive ongoing support and encouragement.

Better yet, when people are aware of one another's strengths, it maximizes their chances of being deployed most effectively. Although this can happen at any time, it is especially helpful when red status updates emerge because individuals can be appropriately brought in based on their relevant strengths.

The "Working Together" Management System also makes sure that following a strengths-based model is an ongoing expectation for the being and doing of leadership. As Alan concludes, "We are committed to lifelong learning and continuous improvement. We are constantly searching for ways to be at our best. We bring the most of who we are to the table every single day. We cannot afford to pursue anything less."

CONCLUDING THOUGHTS

Surprisingly, although we are constantly looking for ways to be at our best, we sometimes overlook one of our key opportunities—leveraging our strengths. The research is overwhelmingly supportive of their effectiveness. By identifying our strengths and putting them into practice, we access the unlimited potential we possess.

CHAPTER 5

MASTERING RECEIVING FEEDBACK

Feedback is the breakfast of champions.
—KEN BLANCHARD

I remember sharing this quote with a long-standing client during a workshop on the science and practice of positive leadership. They had invited a group of high-potential executives to participate in a series of evidence-informed sessions to expand their leadership tool kits. I will never forget when one of the attendees came up to me at the break with a wry smile and remarked, "If feedback truly is the breakfast of champions, why do so few people come to the table when it is served?" We both had a good laugh about this insight.

Although the witty commentary from my workshop participant may seem to ring true, the available research tells a different story. Most people are more interested in *receiving* feedback than they are in *providing* it to others.

These findings map nicely with my own experience and research. When I deliver workshops on the topic of feedback, I often ask the audience to rate their level of openness and interest in receiving feedback from their colleagues. After gathering their answers, I ask the question in a slightly different way: "To what extent are your colleagues open and interested in hearing feedback from you?"

Not surprisingly, while attendees say that they are very open and interested in hearing feedback from their colleagues, they feel much less confident in the opposite scenario. Put simply, they want feedback; other people do not.

You can see how this perception can limit how often we engage in these crucial conversations. We incorrectly assume that our colleagues don't want to receive feedback from us, no matter how well we set the table. This is a fascinating conundrum since most people say they want to hear it.

Before exploring why we should gather and listen to feedback and how to do it effectively, it is important to define the term.

What Is Feedback?

Zenger Folkman, one of the top consulting firms in 360-degree feedback, provided one of the most insightful definitions of feedback I have come across:

Feedback is an interaction between two people where one person has information they believe will be helpful to the (other) person. The giver is motivated by the hope that the message will be understood, accepted, and implemented and will ultimately bring about positive change.[41]

This definition is very rich and has many subtle yet important points. First and foremost, what I really value about this definition is how they frame feedback in terms of how "one person has information they believe will be helpful to the other person." Notice this is from the perspective of the provider, not the receiver. This already gives us a critical insight into why feedback conversations can be so challenging to navigate effectively, whether we are the receiver or the provider.

Another important element is that the giver is "motivated by the hope that the message will be understood, accepted, and implemented and ultimately bring about positive change." No matter how hopeful we are about the potential for positive change, a critical element is the extent to which this message is communicated and received well.

This obstacle is borne out in complementary research into language use. In one compelling survey, researchers discovered that people not only have wildly different interpretations for general terms such as *real possibility* but that this tendency also extends to more obvious examples.

Remarkably, the researchers found that some people do not believe that *always* means "100 percent of the time."[42] With such wide interpretations of seemingly obvious words, are we surprised that there can be considerable variation in more ambiguous and values-laden words such as *respect* or *engagement* when they come up in feedback conversations?

WHY WE SHOULD ORDER A BUFFET BREAKFAST WHEN IT COMES TO FEEDBACK

Our reluctance to offer feedback to others is unfortunate considering the importance of receiving feedback for our success. A separate study conducted by Zenger Folkman revealed that leaders who asked for and acted on feedback were rated as significantly more effective in their roles than their counterparts who did not engage in this powerful practice.[43]

A perfect linear trend emerged: the more leaders asked for and acted on feedback, the more their performance rating improved. On average, leaders who ranked in the top 10th percentile of asking for and acting on feedback were rated in the 90th percentile of leadership effectiveness. If they were in the bottom 10th percentile of this category, on average, they were rated in the 12th percentile of leadership effectiveness. This paints a very compelling case.

I'd like to highlight one final point about this important research. Notice the question. It is asking for *and* acting on feedback. Simply asking for feedback is not enough.

In fact, one of the most powerful things that drives lower engagement in our teams and organizations is to ask for feedback and then do nothing with it. There are two reasons for this.

First, it's a fundamental violation of trust. When someone asks for our opinion, the least we can do is follow up. If we don't, people think we're just going through the motions. We don't really care about their input.

The second reason why failing to act on feedback is so damaging is that we miss an invaluable opportunity to unlock the insights and benefits associated with diverse viewpoints. Our own perspective is often inherently biased. It can be very easy not to see the forest for the trees. We have expectations about how things should and do work, and these beliefs are hard to change. Withholding an outside perspective necessarily limits our ability to draw new connections or chart innovative paths.

SUCCESS STRATEGIES

While the topic of how to receive feedback has admittedly received less research attention, there are powerful insights nonetheless from the available anecdotal and scientific evidence. This section summarizes these best practices so we can capitalize on the learning opportunities that feedback provides.

Start with Why

While this may seem like an insight from Captain Obvious (e.g., why would we be asking for feedback if we didn't have a good reason?), it is an often-overlooked and essential success strategy.

In my coaching work, I stress the importance to my clients of explaining why we want feedback. Unfortunately, sometimes my clients are so excited about the science behind the power of feedback that they skip the step of setting the table properly. In their zeal to get started, they rush in and start asking people feedback questions right away and assume it will go well.

One of my clients, Tim, is a perfect example. He had rarely, if ever, asked for feedback. When he did, he deployed a more rhetorical approach: "Is everything alright with you?" or, "I'm assuming you're happy with how things are going?" These types of questions always rendered the typical response, "All good, boss."

After we discussed the importance of open and honest feedback, we put it on the agenda for our next coaching conversation. Unfortunately, Tim could not contain his curiosity or enthusiasm. He started asking people a series of questions. He thought, *This is such a great idea. What could possibly go wrong?*

As he started asking his team about how he could improve, he was immediately met with blank stares. These were either followed by continued, awkward silence or, "Nothing I can think of. Can I get back to you?" As you can probably guess, nobody did.

Although Tim wanted to surprise me with what he learned at the start of our next session, when we met, he was quite deflated. He could not understand why this strategy, which had so much promise, had not worked for him. Where did he go wrong?

I asked him to look at it from the perspective of his employees. He had not asked for their input about his performance for a very long time. The last time he could recall was a 360-degree feedback exercise from a few years ago, which he openly criticized. He realized how this laid the groundwork for their hesitation and avoidance.

Furthermore, although *he* knew why he was asking for feedback, how could his teammates and colleagues possibly know? We also discussed what their potential reaction could be. I asked him directly to consider what they might be thinking.

After sitting back and reflecting on this for a moment, it suddenly clicked. Tim realized that his team might be worried he would get even with them somehow if they revealed their concerns to him. Also, they were likely wondering, *Why now? He never expressed an interest in this before.* Although it was a desirable and positive change, it seemingly came out of nowhere.

Tim also realized they were unclear about what he was actually looking for. Asking people how he was doing sounded good in theory, but without any further direction from him, his approach was rife with problems. For example, he realized he wasn't being clear on the specific areas in which he wanted feedback or how his team could best frame their feedback in the most constructive way possible.

After our debrief, Tim shared his revelation about the importance of starting with why. He didn't realize how quickly and powerfully a well-intentioned feedback conversation could go off the rails without it.

EXECUTIVE COACHING CASE STUDY: SETTING THE TABLE FOR THE BREAKFAST OF CHAMPIONS

Sally was undoubtedly a high-potential executive within her global organization and was poised to take more responsibility on the international stage. Her employer firmly believed in the importance of providing support to their rising stars, and I was brought in to coach her to the next level.

When we met, she was very excited about the prospect of working with me, particularly in terms of opening the door to receive valuable feedback about her and her approach. In our first meeting, we talked about how this could be a wonderful opportunity for her to obtain feedback from various stakeholder groups, including her employees, peers, supervisor, and clients. As a result, we worked on various scripts she could leverage. Although adapted for each individual, here is the crux of the message:

I just started working with an executive coach, Craig Dowden. As part of our work together, I am asking everyone in my circle for feedback on my performance: areas where I am doing well and areas where I could make improvements. As an invaluable colleague, I really respect you and your insights. In order for me to be at my best, I need to get feedback from people I trust and who observe and experience my behavior in different ways. I have too many biases and habits to do this effectively, and I need your help.

My goal is to create a positive, respectful, and engaging environment where people can truly thrive, where we have courageous conversations and support one another in being at our best. So if in any meeting, project, or conversation, you see something where you feel I am doing a great job or, better yet, can improve, please let me know.

The best way to do this is to pull me aside right away and let me know you're taking me up on my offer to receive feedback from you. Then, get straight to the point. Don't sugarcoat anything. I strongly prefer just to get to the heart

*of the matter rather than spend time saying nice
things before we get to it.*

*What do you think? Can you help me
with this?*

As you can probably guess, Sally received an overwhelmingly positive reaction to this type of framing.
People immediately shared their appreciation about
how she explained why she wanted the feedback, what
type of feedback she was looking, and how they could
best deliver it. They also felt grateful that she saw them
as invaluable to the process. Hearing that spoken out
loud felt great. While we may assume this is obvious,
explicitly stating this fact is quite powerful. Think of
a situation where someone says, "I love you" versus
someone saying, "You know how I feel."

She also received timely and specific feedback, both
constructive and critical, which helped her improve.
Everyone, including her supervisors and external
stakeholders, acknowledged the prompt and profound
changes they observed in her behavior. After receiving
feedback, Sally thanked each person for trusting her
with this information and also followed up with what
she did to address it.

The benefits of her approach were also recognized
by others in her organization, including her peers. They
started following her lead. What's more, Sally was put
on an even faster track for advancement. She quickly
became the North American lead and eventually took

on a coveted role in their Global Strategic Advisory Committee.

Although she felt she had been open to feedback in the past, she shared that making this subtle yet powerful shift in her approach uncovered so much more valuable information and also deepened the quality of her relationships with everyone around her.

Expect Disagreement

If there's one thing for certain, it's that disagreement is everywhere. Ironically, we expect it in countless areas of our lives yet think nothing of it. A great example is going to the movies. While some audience members feel this is an Oscar-worthy, transformative picture, others will not see it nearly as positively—or even see it as a complete waste of time.

This is a good analogy to apply when it comes to receiving personal feedback. While one person may find us approachable, another may describe us as standoffish. Not surprisingly, we also like the person who says we are more approachable than the other person.

Unfortunately, rather than embrace these differences, we can use them as a way to disregard the negative feedback and agree with the perspective that puts us in a positive light. Our rationale is that the positive feedback is closer to the "truth," while the critical feedback is an outlier.

It is essential to remind ourselves that disagreement does not draw into question the validity of the feedback. Quite the opposite: it adds to its richness. When faced with these discrepancies, ask yourself the following questions:

- ▶ Do I act consistently with these different individuals?
- ▶ What words/behaviors might be interpreted differently by these individuals?
- ▶ What opportunities exist to adjust my approach?
- ▶ To what extent am I comfortable with these different perspectives of my behavior?

Seek First to Understand

Another major obstacle we face when receiving feedback well is that it tends to be wrapped in generic language. Rather than provide specifics, people use generic words and adjectives to convey their observations.

We can build on the previous example to drive this point home. Let's take the word *approachable*. Although it is a commonly used word, when we think about it, there can be a variety of behaviors that contribute to us seeming approachable or not. Further, the label of *approachable* can also be a trigger word. Borrowing from the insightful work of Stone and Heen,[44] if we see being approachable as core to our personal and professional identity, we can react defensively against the "accusation" that we are unapproachable.

Rather than reacting strongly or dismissing feedback that's hard to accept, try putting on your curiosity hat. Ask clarification questions and explore what message the person is trying to convey.

In this specific example, ask probing questions such as:

▶ Can you give me some recent examples of when I was unapproachable?

▶ What could I have done differently?

Approaching your feedback journey in this way maximizes the chances you will benefit from the valuable perspectives of others.

It's a Moment in Time

Another obstacle to receiving feedback well is that we can see it as a permanent indictment of our character (or lack thereof). When viewed this way, we can be highly reluctant to accept feedback. An important shift in our mindset can assist us. More accurately, the feedback we are given represents a moment (or even moments) in time. They do not dictate or guarantee things will remain the same. We play the primary role in shaping how we behave in the future. If the feedback is concerning, we can take steps immediately to address it.

The Choice Is Yours!

I will close this section by once again referencing the groundbreaking work of Doug Stone. When I spoke with him, he mentioned that an important consideration to remember is that we always have the choice of what we do with the feedback. We can agree or disagree with the assessments and then decide to do something about it (or not). Just because people provide us with suggestions for how we can improve does not mean we have to do anything with this information.

We can choose to continue on our original path. However, we now are equipped with the knowledge of how our words or behaviors are being perceived by other individuals in our network. Rather than being frustrated by their responses, we can choose to accept the consequences and understand where their reactions are coming from.

Bestselling author Doug Stone cowrote *Thanks for the Feedback*, one of the most impactful and important books I've read on receiving feedback. When I spoke with him about why he and Sheila Heen wrote this book, here's what he had to say:

When we asked people about their most difficult conversations, giving and receiving feedback is always at the top of the list. However, when we looked at the books available, almost all of them focused on how to give feedback effectively. While this is undoubtedly an important skill, we noticed that no matter how well we trained someone in the art of delivering feedback, the person on the other end of the conversation is ultimately more important because they interpret what is being said and decide whether to do anything about it.

Their groundbreaking work uncovered three primary reasons why people resist receiving feedback. The first surrounds the extent to which the receiver feels the feedback is truthful. This relates to any unhelpful or untrue comments that are baked into the feedback that can cause the receiver to reject it outright. For example, if the feedback is delivered poorly in terms of tone or specificity, the receiver can dismiss it despite its accuracy.

Another example is that the feedback includes one untruthful example in a set of observations. Because one aspect is inaccurate, the receiver excludes the rest of the feedback. This is a great example of throwing the proverbial baby out with the bathwater.

Stone gave me an outstanding piece of advice for facing this situation. He suggested, "Rather than asking what's *wrong* with the feedback, we would be far better served to ask what is *right* about it."

The second set of triggers involves who is delivering the feedback and/or the quality of the relationship at the time the feedback is being provided. If the person is someone we dislike or are in conflict with, this can undermine our trust in their motivations, once again leading us to dismiss their insights outright.

The final set of triggers involves our identity, which happens when we perceive the feedback to be less about our behaviors and more about who we are (e.g., our character). This can lead us to lash out and react defensively, which limits or undermines our ability to hear the message.

A wonderful way to counteract this tendency is to shift our mindset into a more growth-oriented perspective. We can ask questions to better understand what the feedback is about. If someone accuses us of being disrespectful, rather than react angrily to their observation, ask them to provide specific examples of when they observed this.

This is very difficult to do in practice and requires us to be very aware of our emotional state. However, as discussed in chapter 3, mastering our emotions is one of the hallmarks of effective leadership. It is virtually impossible to be at our best when we are emotionally hijacked. Taking a more mindful and reflective approach better serves us, in both the short and long run.

CEO MASTERCLASS WITH ALAN MULALLY: ON MASTERING RECEIVING FEEDBACK

Receiving feedback well is a critical aspect of executive excellence. To be at our best, we need to have an accurate understanding of how the world sees us. Just as we would want an honest review of a new product or service, we need the same level of candor when it comes to our leadership and impact.

The "Working Together" Management System is firmly built on a culture of feedback. For starters, the BPR meetings provide a consistent feedback loop. As Alan observes, "When looking at the reds, yellows, and greens, we understand exactly what is going on. We aren't afraid of the information; we embrace it because it informs us about what we need to do, both now and in the future. Feedback is empowerment."

The preeminent focus on feedback ties into an undying belief in the importance of self-awareness. We all have awareness opportunities. "You need to have a really accurate view of yourself when we are "Working Together." To do this requires feedback from the people around you. It's virtually impossible to get this insight on your own. You need to make sure your view of yourself matches up with others' views of you. It's about maximizing your self-awareness."

In "Working Together," every area of the business provides feedback in terms of how the team goes about accomplishing the One Plan. The team uses multiple metrics to ensure there is not a myopic view wherein one group is being highlighted at the expense of another.

"We obtain feedback on all performance measures, including financial, customer satisfaction, employee engagement, and all relevant stakeholder data," Alan says. "Profitable Growth for All truly means *everyone*."

The underlying philosophy adopted about feedback maximizes its effectiveness and impact. It is not viewed negatively. In fact, it is the exact opposite. Feedback is framed as a growth opportunity. It's a sign of caring. If people care about our success, they will share things, both positive and negative. Praise is freely given, as is constructive feedback. Only then can the power of "Working Together" truly be unlocked. Since everyone is aware that the goal is to support each other, the mindset people have about feedback shifts as well. Alan adds, "The observations are seen as less threatening and more empowering. Feedback is a pathway to success versus a road to failure."

Careful consideration is also placed on how feedback is provided, with a particular focus on respect. This is nonnegotiable for Alan. "You have to be so thoughtful about others' dignity when providing feedback. This is the responsibility we have to each other when 'Working Together.' We are committed to lifting them up. Our ultimate goal is to make them better because everyone benefits when that happens. It best serves the individual as well as the team."

One of the primary reasons why "Working Together" provides a Masterclass in receiving feedback well is how it is structured and operationalized. While many companies create periodic or irregular feedback opportunities at best, the genius of "Working Together" is its cadence. Every week, every member of the executive team gets exposed to real-time data through the BPR. "Everyone welcomes the feedback when we are "Working Together." It is not only valued but also encouraged, expected, and appreciated."

This ongoing feedback loop ensures we are consistently exercising our feedback muscles, both in delivering and receiving it. This constant practice also keeps egos in check. Leaders must be comfortable being open to contrarian views. The "Working Together" Management System provides daily opportunities to test the boundaries of our egos.

The frequency of feedback interactions does not solely benefit those on the receiving end. It also effectively reinforces the practice. When people receive feedback from someone, the expectation is that they will give a thank-you. This is an incredibly powerful practice because it rewards the person who is delivering the feedback. Rather than prompt a defensive reaction, it sparks one of gratitude. It signals to the giver and receiver that this is a positive leadership practice. With continuous practice receiving and providing feedback effectively, we get better and more comfortable with these contributions.

To instill this type of feedback culture, everyone is encouraged and expected to ask for feedback from one another. In fact, people ask for feedback from their peers on how they can improve. Alan shares a couple of great feedback questions: "What are a couple of things that I could do to enhance my performance in your eyes?" or, "How can I bring my performance to the next level?" or, "Where do you think I could contribute more?"

Alan makes a compelling case for how the benefits of the Principles and Practices of the "Working Together" Management System apply in all aspects of our lives, including our families. "Say to your significant other, 'I would like to be the best partner I could possibly be for you. What are two or three things I could do?' You can use the same type of question with your children. Imagine the impact this would have on our relationships if we approached them in this way."

Powerful and inspiring questions indeed!

CONCLUDING THOUGHTS

We are well served when we prioritize receiving feedback well. Otherwise, we run the risk of having a biased and inaccurate view of ourselves and our impact.

Feedback is not our enemy; it is our friend. It is at the heart of maximizing our own potential while also supporting those around us to achieve theirs.

CHAPTER 6

MASTERING DIFFICULT CONVERSATIONS

*Anybody can become angry—that is easy; but
to be angry with the right person, and to the
right degree, and at the right time, and for the
right purpose, and in the right way—that is not
within everybody's power and is not easy.*

—ARISTOTLE

When it came to the business they had started
together, Chris and Jenna were each responsible for a different area, but they routinely needed to
collaborate on creating joint solutions for their clients.
In this instance, they had met with a prospect who

asked them to submit a written proposal by 4:00 p.m. the following Tuesday.

It was at this point that the seeds of conflict were sown. Chris was notoriously late submitting materials—so much so that it had already created a significant strain on his personal and professional relationship with Jenna. With the deadline looming, Jenna worried that Chris wouldn't submit his work on time. As the clock ticked closer to the deadline, and per his custom, no emails were forthcoming from Chris letting her know when she could expect his part of the proposal. By Tuesday at noon, with only four hours left to turn in their proposal, she gave up and wrote the entire proposal herself, stamped *Draft* on the cover page, and sent it to the client, copying Chris on the email.

Ten minutes later, she received an angry phone call from Chris, accusing her of "throwing him under the bus" and "making him look bad in front of the client." Worse still, "she clearly wasn't a team player anymore."

As odd as it may seem, both Chris and Jenna are right. Here's the catch: each of them is using a different definition of team player. If you step back and look at it from Jenna's perspective, she understood the risks of doing this herself, but with the deadline only hours away, she thought she was being the ultimate team player by taking care of the proposal and sending it on time. In fact, she felt she was doing the lion's share of the work and saving face for Chris by putting *both* of their names on the document—a far cry from throwing him under the bus. She had also purpose-fully written the word *Draft* on the document and told the client that they welcomed feedback, which she felt was the ultimate safety net.

If you look at the situation through the eyes of Chris, you would see a different picture. In his world, you *never* submit anything before engaging your partner. This makes the other person look bad. When you're on a team together, nothing is more important than presenting a united front.

This is a terrific, real-life example of a difficult conversation.

AN INTRODUCTION TO DIFFICULT CONVERSATIONS

What makes difficult conversations, well, so difficult? When I pose this question in my workshops, I receive a consistent set of answers:

- ▶ There's a lot at stake for people.
- ▶ Our egos or emotions are heavily involved and we take things personally.
- ▶ People are worried how raising this issue may harm the relationship and/or hurt the other person's feelings.
- ▶ It feels easier to ignore the issue than to deal with it head-on.
- ▶ We worry that the conflict is either our fault or exists only in our imagination

▶ We don't have the skills to do it well.

These reasons shed a lot of light on the major elements of a "crucial conversation" and were explained in depth by the authors of *Crucial Conversations*.[45] Four major reasons complicate the landscape when we attempt to have these discussions:

1. **The stakes are high for everyone involved.** If nobody cared about the issue, a difficult conversation would not be necessary.
2. **There are varying opinions on the issue.** If everyone agreed on the issue at hand, there would be nothing difficult to discuss.
3. **Our emotions tend to be triggered.** When the stakes are high and there are differing views on a situation, emotional hijacking is both likely and complicating.
4. **There are potentially significant conse-quences.** These consequences can meaning-fully impact the lives of the individuals—real or imagined. The point is that we see a negative future lying ahead if we do not dig in.

According to research out of Stanford University, when CEOs were asked to identify an area in which they most needed to develop, how to successfully navigate difficult conversations came out on top. This is fascinating considering their position in an organization. Other than the board to whom they report, CEOs occupy the highest authority in their companies, yet they still struggle with this skill. If those in the corner office are concerned about their capacity to effectively engage, it is little wonder that other (aspiring) executives are hesitant to tackle these conversations.

THE POWER OF STORY

The power of story is something that's particularly relevant to difficult conversations. In fact, it may be the most important part. It's the primary reason I used the story of Chris and Jenna to start the chapter.

Yet you can apply this idea of story—the stories we tell ourselves about ourselves, the stories we tell ourselves about other people, and the stories we tell ourselves about our environment—to other situations as well.

One of the complicating factors in all of this is that each of us has a different view of reality. Our personal stories dramatically impact our experiences. I see this all the time in my coaching practice.

The Ladder of Inference

One of the most powerful and practical models to illuminate how we write our own reality comes from the ladder of inference. This concept was introduced by Chris Argyris, a highly respected organizational psychologist, and unpacks the largely unconscious thought process that moves us from an observation to an action.[46] The brilliance of the model is that it simplifies and illuminates each step on our journey, and it is a wonderful application of the power of story.

Although each of us can start out by observing the same data in our world, immediately following the event, we start shaping that narrative through our personal lens. While we may continue to believe that our story is indeed reality, this filtering process continues to impact us. It is akin to the telephone game we played as kids. After the first person in the chain shares a message with the next child, the content starts changing right away. When the message finally gets passed to the end of the line, it often hardly represents what we started with.

A final point is important here. This process not only impacts our story in the current moment, it continues to influence our worldview after the fact. This highlights why being aware of how our minds create our reality is such a powerful tool, not just for navigating conflict but for navigating our entire personal and professional lives as well.

Our Stories Are the Tip of the Iceberg

While our stories mean everything to us, a considerable amount of data is missing. Remember the ladder of inference. Other people, as do we, *select* certain data points for processing. This means they have only a slice of our whole pie.

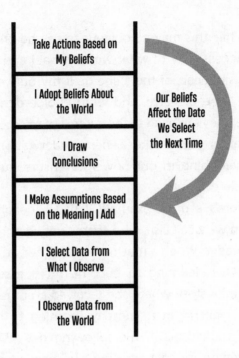

Several years ago, a beautiful photo went viral. It showed the tip of an iceberg, with a substantially larger portion stretching out under the surface. This explains why boats can unexpectedly crash and even sink; only part of the danger is visible to the captain on the surface, but this is much smaller than the danger lurking below.

I think the image of the iceberg is a wonderful metaphor for a difficult conversation. I see the entire iceberg. I have the full picture of the issue. I am aware of what I am saying and, hopefully, what I'm doing. I also know the subtext of my communication—the message behind the message, what I may be trying not to say. What is under the surface.

While this may be obvious to us, the other person has access only to what we have said and done (e.g., the visible part of the iceberg). If my outward appearance, tone of voice, and word choice denote acceptance, they are blind to the subtext of my message (e.g., the larger part of the iceberg underwater). We must do everything in our power to ensure they see the complete picture.

Here's a great example. I had a coaching client, whom we'll call Lisa, who scored very highly as a positive leader. When I met her, one of her development areas was learning to become more assertive. She recalled a story where she received an urgent request from a client on a Tuesday morning to meet with them midafternoon the following day (Wednesday). To prepare for that meeting, she needed one of her top employees (we'll call him Gavin) to pull together some information on the file. Lisa had some time over her lunch hour, which gave her more than sufficient opportunity to get ready.

Gavin was a superstar due to his intellect and responsiveness. He would thoughtfully respond the following morning whenever he received a request. He was doing such a great job that lately Lisa had started providing him with a lot of additional work. He loved the increased responsibility that came with a larger client load and was thriving. Lisa didn't want to put undue pressure on Gavin, so she sent him a note letting him know about the meeting and asked him to get her the information "as soon as possible." Given his past performance, she was sure she would get it the following morning at the latest.

As the day progressed, she saw Gavin busily scurrying around the office. As always, she was amazed and impressed by his level of energy.

She asked, "How is everything going?"

He replied, "Great! Really making terrific progress on things." She was excited to see what he came back with.

The next morning, Lisa's inbox was still empty. That was odd, but she knew she could count on Gavin. Midmorning arrived, and there was still no word. As lunchtime waned and her meeting time approached, she sent Gavin a panicked text in all caps that read, "WHERE IS THE INFORMATION? I AM MEETING THE CLIENT IN LESS THAN AN HOUR."

She went into the meeting without the information and stumbled her way through. She apologized for her lack of preparedness and said she would rectify the situation as soon as possible.

Feeling disappointed and angry, she couldn't understand how Gavin had let her down. This was a new account and represented a large opportunity. Although it was a small initial project, the potential was big if certain things fell into place. This definitely set them back a lot.

When she spoke with Gavin, she shared her disappointment with him. She asked him how he could possibly leave her blowing in the wind without that vital information. She had grown to count on him, and now this threw everything into question.

Gavin sat back, stunned at this revelation. He expressed his shock at the all-caps text. She had never spoken to him like that before. He then handed her an immaculate dossier on their largest client. He had been tirelessly working on that project for weeks and had remembered Lisa saying, "No matter what is going on, this has to be your top priority. This client will make or break us, and it has to receive maximum effort." Although Lisa had given him a deadline of tomorrow, Gavin knew the client liked receiving things early so he'd doubled down to make sure it was completed.

Stepping back, we can clearly see how this situation went off the rails. The tip of the iceberg for Lisa's request was, "Can you get me this information on Client X as soon as you can?" The message below the surface, which Lisa felt uncomfortable communicating, was, "But I need this by noon tomorrow so I can be ready for the meeting at 2:00 p.m."

Notice that Gavin did not have access to any of that information. In his mind, he was asked to get Lisa some information for an emerging client as soon as he could. Given her directive to make their largest client his top priority, the soonest he could get to it was Wednesday afternoon. He also did not know Lisa was meeting with this emerging client the next day. Remember, those details were left out.

As Lisa and I unpacked the situation, she could clearly see how what was left unsaid not only derailed the project but undermined the trust and strength of her relationship with Gavin.

Challenge Your Assumptions

One common and unfortunate situation I come across in my coaching work is difficult conversations that have not taken place. When I explore this question with clients, they have numerous examples at the ready. When I ask them to explain what has prevented them from addressing the issue, I get some version of, "They can't handle the conversation."

When I hear this, I ask, "How do you *know* that?" This question is often met with a perplexed pause and sometimes an exasperated, "I just know, okay?" As I continue exploring for evidence to support their belief, they cannot recall a previous conversation where they tried to raise the issue or observed the colleague in question react poorly to someone else. Yet their steadfast belief that they "know" what will happen remains.

Unfortunately, we all too often put the blame on the other person without having any evidence to support it. Worse still, we employ this blame game because *we* are unprepared and uncomfortable with the conversation rather than the other way around.

Step One: Identify Unaddressed Conflicts

Think about a difficult conversation you feel would be important to have but believe the other person cannot handle it.

Step Two: Examine the Quality of Your Evidence

For each of these conversations, take a close, hard look at the evidence you have to support your belief. Ask yourself:

- Have I really tried to raise this issue before and been met with a hostile or poor reaction?
- Have I really seen others attempt to raise another (similar) issue that went poorly?

Step Three: Explore a Pathway

If your answers to these two questions are *no*, ask yourself what are *you* afraid of about having this conversation.? How can you prepare to engage in a conversation with this person?

Although these may be uncomfortable questions to ponder, the value of answering them is extraordinary.

I would like to make one final important observation. I find that in the vast majority of cases when we have not initiated a difficult conversation with someone, we treat them as if we already did and the conversation went poorly. In other words, we judge them for a discussion that we didn't even give them a chance to participate in.

PREPARING FOR DIFFICULT CONVERSATIONS

CEOs and other senior leaders widely recognize that being strategic is a crucial competency for their success. A recent *Harvard Business Review* article cited a study of sixty thousand executives from more than one hundred and forty countries. When they were asked what leadership behaviors were critical to their future success, 97 percent selected the capacity to be strategic.[47]

Yet, despite our preoccupation with strategic thinking, very few of us employ it when it comes to the most important conversations of our lives. Here's a simple thought experiment that illustrates this point. How often have you sat down and prepared for a difficult conversation, either professionally or personally? If you're like most people, the honest answer is . . . not that often.

If we enter these conversations without being grounded, the potential for derailment is high. We can also minimize or even miss an opportunity to create a substantial turning point for repairing or strengthening a relationship. Here are some critical elements to consider when gauging our preparedness for a difficult conversation:

First, ask yourself, *Am I emotionally ready?* This is a crucial first question. How are we feeling about the upcoming discussion? Anxious anticipation is good; profound dread is not. We must work through our emotions so that we are in the best possible space to engage with someone else. We have to be ready before they can be.

Second, ask yourself, *What are the most important things I want to cover during this conversation?* Rather than leave this to chance or our memories, write down these core messages and bring them with you to the conversation. Many of my clients make a favorable and positive impact by sharing their intention with the other person. For example, they say something such as, "You may notice I have some notes that I will refer to from time to time. This conversation is very important to me, and I want to make sure I don't miss anything.

As you can probably guess, this sends a powerful message to the other person in terms of how much emphasis you have placed on getting this right. It also reveals that you have spent time thinking about this in advance, which shows that you likely won't be tripped up by anything unexpected. These underlying messages are invaluable in difficult conversations.

Third, identify the context. There are times when the seeds of conflict are sown through text messages or emails. Although it may be enticing to continue in that medium, it's essential to hold these conversations in an environment that is as information-rich as possible— and that is either face-to-face or in a videoconference (cameras on!). The vast majority of how we assign meaning to a message comes from nonverbal cues, such as tone of voice and body language. This means if we choose to engage in a difficult conversation via text, the chances of it going well are significantly reduced. Although it may seem the most straightforward and least invasive option at first, we will spend considerably more time dealing with the fallout of our choice for hitting the easy button.

Fourth, on top of your core messages, it is important to consider what desired outcome you want at the end of the conversation. This does not mean that everything is resolved entirely; it is more about what has been decided and what the next steps are (if any). As the old saying goes, "If you don't know where you're going, any road will get you there." Be mindful about the destination for the conversation so you can effectively steer it in that direction. As an example, if something extraneous gets introduced, you can more effectively put it in the parking lot and come back to it later.

By reflecting on these strategies, you can more effectively prepare yourself for what lies ahead. It is essential to reimagine your relationship with difficult conversations. Rather than see them as uncomfortable and pointless, view them as powerful and important opportunities to build stronger relationships and communication with the people you care about most.

"D" IS FOR PREPARATION

In his book *Perfecting Your Pitch*, bestselling author and negotiation expert Ronald Shapiro outlines a simple yet powerful system that can be applied to successfully navigate difficult conversations. He calls his system "The Three Ds." When I spoke with him about his approach, he provided some additional context.

Drafting

The first step is Drafting; there are two objectives here. "One is to get as much of the message down in advance as you can. This makes sure you will not forget anything when the conversation happens," Shapiro said. "And second, if you're in an emotional or tense situation, it allows you to get those feelings on paper. The very act of expressing these feelings helps us get rid of some of these emotions."

Devil's Advocacy

In the Devil's Advocacy stage, we are thinking about how our counterpart will receive our message, no matter how well intended it may be. What will they be hearing or not hearing? What emotions or assumptions may they be bringing to the table? What are their primary areas of concern that we may be missing or minimizing in articulating our position? These are critical questions to ask because they get us out of our chair and allow us to take a more objective vantage point when evaluating our draft.

Although the Devil's Advocacy stage can be done on our own, Shapiro strongly advises engaging one or more trusted people in our network to assist us during this stage. Given their relative objectivity, this maximizes the chances that they will identify things we may miss. Our personal needs or biases may blind us to important pieces of information.

Deliver

The final stage is Deliver, which involves practicing a pitch in front of an audience. This can be as simple as reading it out loud to yourself or, ideally, enlisting some or all of your devil's advocates. This creates an opportunity to hear and test our messages in real time and ensure our delivery matches our desired impact.

When we practice our delivery, it is important to remember not to make it sound mechanical. We want to deliver our message as naturally as possible so we can anticipate how the other person may react. It also allows us to get comfortable sharing our story out loud.

If you're still wondering why you should bother to prepare for difficult conversations, Mr. Shapiro shared a powerful metaphor: "I remind [my clients] of pilots. They are very smart and capable individuals who clearly know how to fly a plane. However, before every flight, each one of them checks their preparation checklist because they do not want to make a mistake. If pilots do this, why shouldn't we?"

SUCCESS SECRETS TO DIFFICULT CONVERSATIONS

Given the importance of mastering difficult conversations, we should give careful attention to the following tools and techniques so we can navigate them more effectively.

Address Right Away

In chapter 3 we saw that one of the key steps to developing resilience is to acknowledge our emotions, particularly our feelings of stress. If we avoid these, they can grow far bigger over time.

The same holds true of difficult conversations. If someone we know is saying or doing something that is negatively affecting us, address it right away when it is small. Otherwise, it becomes increasingly difficult to raise. If left for too long, we may boil over and go on the attack. Or we may build up such strong, negative feelings around it that we may walk away from the relationship without providing the other person with an opportunity to fix things.

Ask Lots of Questions

In my experience, a key factor that extends or intensifies a conflict is when the other person doesn't feel heard. It is less about the ultimate path forward and more about whether the other party demonstrates any interest in what we have to say.

Asking questions accomplishes a lot of positive outcomes. First, it exhibits our active curiosity in the other individual's position. In addition, how we frame our question shows how much care and attention we are paying to the situation. Last, but not least, through the power of questions we can gather tremendous insight into the position of the other person. What is important to them? Where are they possibly willing to compromise? What are their non-negotiables? All this information is invaluable in terms of crafting our strategy.

Be Comfortable Starting Over

I often say to my clients, "How a conversation starts impacts how a conversation ends." As mentioned at the start of this chapter, difficult conversations evoke tremendous unease in most people. We are already emotionally triggered at the thought of the conversation, let alone engaging in it. Despite our best intentions and even preparation, we can have a false start. We can awkwardly blurt out something or poorly phrase one of our key points right at the beginning of the exchange. This can set things off course before we even begin.

Although we may feel like the ship has already left the harbor and there's nothing we can do now, nothing could be further from the truth. We can also hit the reset button.

Imagine you said something that clearly and immediately created a reaction in the other person. Rather than continue, you could pause and say, "I'm sorry. I feel I didn't say that as clearly or carefully as I should have. Can we start over? I want this to be a constructive conversation, and I don't feel I did my part effectively."

By taking the opportunity to reset the conversation, we maximize the chances for a positive outcome.

Remember, the Road to Hell Is Paved with Good Intentions

This is one of the biggest derailers in difficult conversations.

Unfortunately, we tend to assess our words and behaviors based on our intentions. They are highly visible to us. Whenever we say or do something, we intimately and innately understand our motivations.

The other person assesses our words and behaviors through their personal, preexisting filter. That means it's not what we do or say but how they *experience* what we do or say that matters.

When we say or do something that has an unintended impact, we can react defensively. How could the person think we would ever treat them this way? This is a highly ineffective response and can escalate the conflict.

It is important to remember that although we know our intentions, the other person does not. It is vital to remain curious and respectful as we explore what

went wrong. This is valuable for addressing the immediate conflict while also equipping us with invaluable
information about what not to do in the future.

THE POWER OF A POSITIVE NO

William Ury is the author of multiple bestsellers and
is a cofounder of the Program on Negotiation at
Harvard University. He is widely recognized as one
of the world's leading authorities on negotiation and
mediation, having taught courses to tens of thousands of corporate executives, labor leaders, diplo-
mats, and military officers around the world.

Over the past thirty-five years, Ury has acted
as a negotiator and mediator to navigate the most
intense conflict situations, including ethnic wars in
the Middle East, the Balkans, the former Soviet Union,
and Colombia.

Although many people know of his books
Getting to Yes and *Getting Past No*, the third book in
this trilogy, *The Power of a Positive No*, provides an
extraordinarily valuable framework that empowers
us to successfully navigate difficult conversations.

As Ury indicates, *no* is one of the most important
and powerful words in any language. Unfortunately,
most of us are so uncomfortable saying it, we create
or exacerbate conflict with others as a result. This
generally results from three of our typical responses
to the specter of saying *no*:[48]

1. We **accommodate** the request, which is another way of saying we don't say *no* to someone when we should. In this case, we begrudgingly agree to doing something that we don't want to do.
2. We **attack** the other person as a means of immediately shutting down the conversation. We channel our own discomfort about the prospect of saying *no* and take it out on the other person.
3. We **avoid** saying anything at all. This happens in cases where we hope the other person will "forget about it," "not ask me again," or "take care of it themselves."

Each of these responses, although popular, is not very effective. Ury provides a better way: a simple, straightforward process that allows us to respect our needs as well as the needs of the other person involved.

1. **Start with yes.** Although this may sound counterintuitive, it is an incredibly important and often overlooked step. It is likely the most common mistake we make when we want to say no. The heart of this step is to ensure we validate the other person.
2. **Share our no.** While important to acknowledge the other person, we must remember that we are an equal partner in this

relationship. This allows us to speak our truth as well. It's not about attacking the other person. It is about clarifying what is important to us.

3. **End with an invitation to yes.** This is where we engage with the other person to identify a mutually satisfactory path forward. We can either leave it as an open question or propose an alternative and seek their acceptance.

Consider an example that involves a situation with a direct report. Imagine one of your employees walked into your office right after lunch and asked to meet with you about something they were working on. You have an urgent deadline of 4:00 p.m. that afternoon for a high-profile project for the CEO. Here is the power of a positive no:

- **Start with yes:** "I appreciate the fact that you really want to see me right now ..."
- **Follow with no:** ". . . but I am working on an urgent file that is due at 4:00 p.m. today."
- **End with a proposed yes:** "When is a good time for us to meet tomorrow?"

You may be thinking that this situation is easier to navigate since it is one of your employees and you may feel more empowered to stand your ground. What about when it involves one of your superiors? Consider this example.

You are the senior vice president of sales for a large corporation. At noon on Tuesday, your boss asks you to review a large client proposal by 9:00 a.m. the next day. You are already working on several urgent files, including some they assigned you a few weeks back. Here's how you can approach it:

- **Start with yes:** "I appreciate how important it is to get this done by tomorrow morning."
- **Follow with no:** "I am working on several urgent projects that are also due tomorrow, including the Smith file you asked me to do a few weeks back."
- **End with a proposed yes:** "What is my top priority?" or "How should I approach this?" or "Should I move the Smith file until later this week since we don't meet the client until next Tuesday?"

As you can see from these examples, there are countless applications of this model. The power rests in its ability to honor ourselves *and* the other person involved. Think about different situations you are facing and explore how you might apply the principles.

CEO MASTERCLASS WITH ALAN MULALLY: ON MASTERING DIFFICULT CONVERSATIONS

Navigating important and seemingly difficult conversations is a necessary and critical part of who you need to be and what you need to do as a leader. There will be times when people have profound differences of opinion about an issue, and what is ultimately decided may impact all the participants in significant ways. These situations can derail important conversations and drive disconnection and conflict.

One of the best ways to navigate difficult conversations is to create a safe environment where you can talk about the most challenging subjects without emotions boiling over. The "Working Together" Management System creates this environment and supports this culture. As Alan says, "When we are very clear about the expected behaviors, the conversation is not really that difficult. When we respect each other's dignity, we can discuss anything, no matter the stakes."

Another crucial element of "Working Together" that makes navigating difficult conversations easier is its compelling vision to create value for all the stakeholders and the greater good. "Our focus," says Alan, "is on doing what's best for everyone to accomplish our compelling vision."

A key ingredient to the success of "Working Together" is that there is zero tolerance for behaviors that are not supportive of the system. As Alan explains, "If someone is not supportive of our expected behaviors, we talk with them immediately. This is our unique role and responsibility as leaders—we hold ourselves and our teams accountable to the principles and practices of 'Working Together.' Every participant has to continually decide if they are committed to our 'Working Together' Management System. If they are not, they are deciding to move on. We still love them and wish them the best going forward."

Alan believes the CEO has an even greater role to play when it comes to protecting the sanctity of the "Working Together" Management System. "Although everyone is responsible for 'Working Together,' there is no greater responsibility for the CEO than to keep this front and center."

Another key ingredient of "Working Together" is that difficult conversations are "grounded in facts and data." Using this as a constant frame of reference helps keep emotions in check. This is by design so people can move forward effectively together.

"We approach these conversations by using observable metrics, be it client satisfaction, financial performance, or employee satisfaction. We also bring our leadership behaviors to these conversations. We keep our attention on the data and deliver the message in the most respectful way possible. It's talking about what is going on, either from a performance or behavior perspective. It is not a personal attack. It's highlighting a challenging situation and working together to determine how we go forward."

The impacts of constructing these conversations in this way are profound. As Alan shares, "It is not unusual for someone to thank the other person for raising a difficult issue with them. That's because these conversations are focused on our plan and strategy to deliver our compelling vision."

Rather than create strain within teams, these difficult conversations have the opposite effect. "Our relationships deepen because of these conversations. And it speaks volumes to our potential when we approach things in this way."

Despite these lofty standards, everyone is human. Sometimes we may act out of character or behave inconsistently the Principles and Practices of the "Working Together" Management System. Once again, team members are asked to take responsibility for their actions. Just as they hold one another accountable, they apply the same standards to their personal behavior.

"We all will make mistakes. That's a given. How we react when we make a mistake is critically important. I always remind everyone, when you violate one of these leadership qualities, immediately say you're sorry. Be authentic and sincere. The power of an apology is that you're showing you're a real person and that you're committing to our 'Working Together' Principles, Practices, and Management System going forward."

As was the case with giving and receiving feedback, the regularity of these conversations builds individual and collective abilities for having difficult conversations. People are not as afraid of them anymore. As Alan says, "People look forward to the benefits that will come out of having these conversations with their colleagues rather than being wrapped up by the fear of what could go wrong."

Not surprisingly, this creates an environment where people want to learn, grow, and thrive. "Everyone loves 'Working Together'!" Alan says. "It always works. Who wouldn't want to be part of a team where your dignity is always respected and everyone wants you to do well?"

CONCLUDING THOUGHTS

Difficult conversations are a part of life, personally and professionally. Despite their prevalence, the vast majority of us feel ill-equipped or unwilling to face them. If we want to lead, however, mastering this skill is essential for our success and for having the impact we most desire. We need to respect our boundaries and the boundaries of others. We must navigate complex and complicated issues with a deft and direct approach. Taking the time to ready ourselves for this journey maximizes our chances for success.

CHAPTER 7

MASTERING AUTHENTIC LEADERSHIP

*We need authentic leaders, people of the highest
integrity, committed to building enduring organizations.... We need leaders with the courage
to build their companies to meet the needs
of all their stakeholders, and who recognize
the importance of their service to society.*
—BILL GEORGE, BESTSELLING AUTHOR
OF *AUTHENTIC LEADERSHIP*

Making authentic leadership the focus of the final
chapter was an easy choice. How can we expect
to lead others effectively and successfully if we are
inauthentic? While the case for leading authentically

may seem obvious, putting this into practice can be much more challenging. It represents the culmination and extension of each of the preceding chapters. My goal in closing with this chapter is to challenge you to think differently about authentic leadership and how you live it every day.

THE ONLY THING WE HAVE TO FEAR IS FEAR ITSELF

Over my twenty-five years of experience as an executive coach, I've found the only thing that may exceed the potential of authentic leadership is the fear of practicing it. In countless coaching conversations, my clients express concern and consternation about tapping into who they are when it comes to leadership.

Leaders invariably wonder whether they will be enough. Will their direct reports, stakeholders, and board members respect them if they pull back the curtain and reveal their true selves? This hesitation is grounded in an endless parade of self-doubting questions and behaviors.

Make no mistake. This fear is understandable. Substantial risk is involved. It is much safer to behave and lead based on what others expect of us. That way, if we fall short, it wasn't truly our fault; it was someone else's. But if we fail following our own hearts and minds, we have no one else to blame.

This is the heart of why authentic leadership is so hard and so rare. We are reluctant to take the ultimate risk, to put ourselves out there without a safety net.

As much as fear drives our desire to avoid leading authentically, the rewards are extraordinary when we do. During the beginning stages of the COVID-19 crisis, most of my clients wondered what to do. There was so much uncertainty. Where was the guidebook for how to successfully lead through a global pandemic? They knew everyone in their organization was feeling the same way. What could they do?

When discussing what to share, there were concerns about looking weak. Would people lose confidence in their leadership? How could they comment on things they didn't know about? It seemed like an impossible situation—the definition of being stuck between a rock and a hard place.

In each of my conversations, we discussed how each individual leader could authentically speak their truth. For example, while they couldn't guarantee against the possibility of job losses, they would do everything possible to prevent them. In other cases, although they could not divulge the complete financial picture of the organization, they showed the parts that they could. They shared their personal concerns about possibly contracting COVID-19 and the demands on their time when trying to balance work and family responsibilities at home.

Some of my clients embraced the possibly scary idea of hosting "Ask Me Anything" sessions. Rather than put up a PowerPoint with flashy graphics and colorful data, they removed the safety net from below their leadership high wire and invited their employees to ask them any question they wanted. And boy, did they ever! My clients were asked everything under the sun and learned the extraordinary power and freedom found in the phrase "I don't know."

They didn't lose the respect and engagement of their teams; they actually increased it. They didn't show their shortcomings as a leader; they showcased their humanity. Every time I debriefed one of these transformational pivot points with a client, the message I heard was the same. Here's one of my favorites:

> *That was one of the hardest and most rewarding things that I have ever done. . . . I was overwhelmed by how many positive emails, phone calls, and text messages I received. People said they never felt more inspired. I never felt more afraid. It's amazing how those two go together. It's amazing what happens when you can just let go and be yourself. I will remember this for the rest of my life.*

With that in mind, how do you feel about mastering your authentic leadership? Anxious? Conflicted? Excited? These are all legitimate reactions. I encourage you to continue to sit with these emotions as we journey through this chapter together.

THE BUSINESS CASE FOR AUTHENTIC LEADERSHIP

There is considerable scientific evidence that points to the importance of authentic leadership. Although the concept was first introduced in the 1960s, Bill George spearheaded interest in the concept with his bestselling book *Authentic Leadership*. Since its publication in 2003, research into the topic has exploded. Here is a summary of some key findings:

▶ Authentic leadership was the strongest predictor of job satisfaction for employees. It also had positive impacts on overall attitudes toward work and happiness.[49]

▶ Authentic leadership affects employee innovation. This study was instructive because it involved a cross-cultural sample of organizations. The results revealed that "when business owners are perceived as more authentic leaders, their employees show higher personal initiative and are more engaged at work and, in turn, identify more innovative solutions to be implemented in the organization."[50] Given how innovation is such a critical competitive advantage to the sustainability and ultimate thriving of an organization, the implications of these results are both obvious and important.

▶ The benefits of authentic leadership extend beyond its effects on attitudes, emotions, and creativity. Evidence also indicates it elevates on-the-job performance.[51] One particularly compelling study explored the impacts of authentic leadership within two high-stress occupations—police services and the military.[52] Past research suggested that the role of the leader is especially intensified in these environments. In both cases, authentic leadership behaviors were a significant predictor of having higher-performing employees.

▶ Authentic leadership appears to have the strongest effects on the most disengaged. In a fascinating study, which involved over eight hundred team members and their immediate supervisors, authentic leadership had the most impact on team members with a low sense of psychological capital (the positive and developmental state of an individual characterized by high self-efficacy, optimism, hope, and resiliency).[53] Working for authentic leaders prompted their team members to feel a deeper sense of responsibility to deliver positive outcomes. An added benefit was that the leaders raised their own performance. Given how challenging it has been to effectively address disengaged employees, the implications of this research and the opportunity it presents for organizations is especially important.

▶ The positive impacts of authentic leadership stretch across industries and sectors, including financial services. After an intense examination of the relationship between authentic leadership and trust, particularly in the banking sector, the researchers reported that authentic leaders who are "deeply aware of how they think and behave and are perceived by others as being aware of their own and others' values/moral perspectives, knowledge, and strengths" inspired interpersonal trust between themselves and their direct reports, which also increased levels of work engagement.[54]

▶ In a study involving close to forty companies on the Fortune 1,000 list, researchers found a strong relationship between the perception of CEO authenticity and the level of gender diversity and organizational inclusiveness, with more authentic leaders directing more diverse teams.[55] This connection is notable since research suggests that diversity leads to significantly greater market share, higher levels of both team and corporate performance, and higher-quality decision-making.[56]

▶ The benefits of authentic leadership are not just limited to followers. The leaders themselves experience gains as a result. In a powerful study reported in *Harvard Business Review*, individuals who were more authentic reported experiencing significantly higher levels of job satisfaction, inspiration, and sense of community. On the flip side, authentic individuals were significantly less likely to experience job stress. The researchers argued that the less time and energy people spent on engaging in self-management, the more time and energy they had to invest in work-related tasks.[57]

WHAT IS AUTHENTIC LEADERSHIP?

Now that we understand the business case for authentic leadership, it is important to define it. According to the latest research, authentic leadership is composed of four distinct yet overlapping elements.[58] These include:

▶ **Self-Awareness:** Scientific research has repeatedly demonstrated that leaders who have greater self-awareness perform at a significantly higher level than their counterparts. Knowing who we are and how we come across to others enable us to successfully manage our words and behaviors so we can adapt to our environment much more effectively.

▶ **Relational Transparency:** Leaders who openly discuss their thoughts and feelings achieve high levels of trust and commitment from their employees. Another key advantage is that employees will be more inclined to share their own shortcomings, concerns, and challenges. This is especially advantageous when it comes to project work, where problems are more likely to be identified earlier in the process so that they can be managed and dealt with accordingly. There is nothing worse than finding out about a problem at the eleventh hour that could have been easily dealt with in the early stages.

▶ **Balanced Processing:** This involves seeking out and objectively analyzing different types and sources of information before deciding on a course of action. A simple example would be leaders who ask their direct reports for ideas, opinions, and feedback.

▶ **Internalized Moral Perspective:** Authentic leaders possess a highly defined moral code to which they rigorously adhere. For this reason, these leaders encourage the people they work with to honor and uphold their own values, even if those values run counter to those of the leader. Rather than being seen as messy forms of conflict, differences are celebrated and encouraged to drive better-quality decisions and maximize alignment.

THE POTENTIAL PERILS OF
AUTHENTIC LEADERSHIP

Despite the powerful business case for authentic leadership, if you sit with the idea for a moment, you may begin to question whether there are limits to its application. Let me explain.

Brené Brown, a bestselling author and highly regarded TED speaker, defines authenticity as "the choice to let our true selves be seen."[59] This is insightful because it underlines the intentionality behind the action. We are making a conscious choice to let others see behind the curtain. Although this sounds wonderful in theory, what if being your authentic self in practice means being a jerk?

This is exactly the position that Adam Grant took in a thought-provoking column in the *New York Times*. He argued that "just be yourself" is terrible advice. To make his case, he shared the real-life example of author A. J. Jacobs, who "spent a few weeks trying to be totally authentic. He announced to an editor that he would try to sleep with her if he were single and informed his nanny that he would like to go on a date with her if his wife left him. ... You can imagine how his experiment worked out."[60]

Using this lens, it is easy to see how completely sharing our unedited thoughts, feelings, and observations has the potential to create tremendous harm in our personal and professional relationships.

You may be wondering why I am providing this counterargument: why would I share the data behind the power of authentic leadership only to immediately ask you to question it? The reason is that I want to challenge your notions and assumptions about leadership in general. Leadership is complex and nuanced. There are inherent paradoxes that must be navigated. So you may be reasonably wondering, *What do I do now?*

Unfortunately, what gets in the way of answering this question is that many people feel that being authentic means giving license to being a jerk. Their operating algorithm goes something like this: "Who cares what I say or how I say it, because I am only expressing my authentic self? If someone else has an issue, isn't that their problem?"

This overemphasizes the word *authentic* and diminishes the word *leadership*. Authentic leadership is about adhering to a moral code. It is about doing good to lead well. It is about making the right choices, not the easy ones.

Our responsibility is finding ways to authentically express ourselves—but not at the expense of the other person. We do not need to tear someone else down to stand up for our point of view. We don't need to leave a trail of bodies in our wake to pursue our agenda or our objectives.

The critical question to answer is, *How do I stay true to who I am while honoring the values of the individuals and organizations with whom I interact?*

HOW TO BE AN AUTHENTIC CEO: BESTSELLING AUTHOR BILL GEORGE

When it comes to authentic leadership, Bill George literally wrote the book on it. The author of *True North* and *Authentic Leadership*, George previously served as CEO for Medtronic from 1991 to 2001. During his tenure, he took the company from a market cap of $1 billion to $60 billion.

Prior to his role with Medtronic, George worked for Honeywell, where he was directly in line to become the next CEO. Yet he did not feel comfortable with the company. "I felt like I'd hit a wall . . . I wasn't being myself."[61]

Then he recalls a piece of advice from one of his mentors: "Sometimes you have to take the elevator down a floor to go up." When George learned about Medtronic, it was like a breath of fresh air. "I could be myself and feel the passion, the excitement," he explains. And after two years as COO, he took over as CEO.

He asserts, "Just be yourself. You can't be something else. If you're a tulip, be a tulip. If you're a rose, and you've got some thorns, it's okay. You can produce beautiful buds. But you've got to be who you are. And then bloom from that position."

He also highlights the importance of a moral compass. He argues that an authentic leader is one "whose character was the ingredient that mattered most."[62]

George also emphasizes that authentic leadership is a daily endeavor. "No one can be authentic without failing," George writes. "Everyone behaves inauthentically at times, saying and doing things that they will come to regret. The key is to have the self-awareness to recognize these times and listen closely to colleagues who point them out....This is a lifelong journey in which we are always discovering the next layer."[63]

LIVING AUTHENTIC LEADERSHIP

This chapter has laid out the foundations of authentic leadership and the road to mastery. It has challenged us to think about what it means and why it is important. Before providing some exercises, I am going to talk about the *what* of authentic leadership—the key questions and steps you can take to continue your journey in mastering authentic leadership.

Self-Awareness

Self-awareness is at the heart of mastering authentic leadership. Considerable research documents the critical linkage between self-awareness and individual[64] and corporate success.[65] Here are core ways we can elevate our self-awareness to elevate our authentic leadership:

> ▶ Recognize our mindsets and triggers that can prompt us to adopt a growth or fixed mindset.

▸ Be aware of the factors that can positively or negatively impact our level of resilience.

▸ Identify our strengths and look for ways to capitalize on them more often.

▸ Gather more thoughtful and accurate feedback from the people around us.

▸ Look for difficult conversations we are avoiding and find ways to address them.

Relational Transparency

One of my coaching clients, whom we'll call Stewart, has experienced the power of relational transparency firsthand. He built a very successful company from scratch. From the earliest days, he pulled all-nighters to drive extraordinary results. From the seed of an idea he planted in college, he grew the company to over one hundred employees, and it was attracting investor attention.

Stewart's exceptional intelligence was a double-edged sword. While it allowed him to decide with laser-focus what needed to be done, it intimidated others. This became even more of an issue as the company grew bigger. He also became so accustomed to doing what he wanted that he had difficulty letting go of even minor decisions. Even though he realized he and the company needed feedback and ideas from his team to go to the next level, he had trouble receiving them, even when he directly asked.

This hesitation was compounded by the fact that his resting state seemed brooding. Even when Stewart was relaxed, he had a stern look. When engaged in a conversation, especially about ideas, this was amplified, which gave people the impression he was unhappy or frustrated. What could he do?

This was his authentic self. He did not want to downplay his intelligence or minimize his passion for constructive debate. At the same time, he recognized that he needed others' input to drive their engagement as well as team and organizational performance.

In our coaching work, we discussed the importance of letting people see behind the curtain and how he could provide context to his behaviors. We worked together on a script so he could tell his direct reports that he was very passionate about debating ideas. When he was highly engaged, he realized he could sound dismissive or confrontational. This was not his desire. He wanted (and even needed) people to challenge him.

He also talked about how his resting state appeared stern and even unwelcoming. He wanted his team members to check in and not avoid him for fear of him being in a bad mood. He asked them to let him know when he appeared serious and unapproachable. He also committed to working on smiling more and sharing his feelings so people didn't need to guess about his emotional state.

I spoke with his team after he raised the curtain on his inner world. They expressed profound appreciation for his transparency as well as his invitation to be challenged. They shared that everyone "has their stuff" and they respected how he recognized his problematic behaviors. In turn, they had more confidence in calling him out.

In the following weeks, Stewart noticed a major shift in both his one-on-ones as well as his team meetings. People were more forthcoming with their input and objections. He started to be challenged more often in meetings. He realized he had difficulty adapting to this shift and felt triggered in some circumstances. Rather than keep that inside, he took a risk and told people about it right away. The results were profound. The quality of the decisions increased significantly. A proposal for a major client was successfully pitched as a result of fierce yet respectful debate. Everyone felt like they contributed. Their scores improved across the board, especially on engagement, innovation, and psychological safety.

Stewart was pleasantly surprised with the results. He had no idea how much it would mean to his team to hear about his challenge areas. He didn't realize how much his past behavior had created hesitation with his team.

He encouraged his direct reports to share their own challenge areas with their teams. His leadership team reported back similar gains. The company grew and received a large third-party investment. One of the reasons cited was the power of their culture.

Stewart's story is a powerful illustration of how we can continue to honor our authentic selves without suffering the downside. In his case, his team continued to observe his tendency to exhibit brooding behavior. He would sometimes fall back into old habits and come across as unnecessarily combative and argumentative when debating ideas. The difference was that people now felt empowered to let him know, and he had the opportunity to course correct.

Balanced Processing

To be at our best, we need input from everyone around us. If we are caught in siloed thinking, we run the risk of making poor or uninformed decisions. To move this from idealistic vision to reality, we need to create an environment where this information flows freely. We cannot access the highest-quality insight without focusing on fostering the conditions to receive it.

As leaders, we can ask ourselves very powerful questions to determine how effectively we are showing up in this way.

- ▶ Ask your team members the extent to which they feel psychologically safe to share their ideas and perspectives. Ask them for input on what you say or do that fosters that type of environment. Ask them for their ideas on how you can improve.
- ▶ To what extent do you seek out contrarian points of view? Do you refer to the same people

or sources of information? How comfortable are you with dissenting views?

▶ What mechanisms could you use to assess the quality of your decision-making? Do you have mentors or a board of advisors you could speak with to challenge your thinking?

▶ When was the last time you changed your mind based on someone else's perspective? If you are having trouble answering this question, it may indicate you may have some opportunity for growth.

Internalized Moral Perspective

"We're in a time when we must choose between what is right and what is easy."

Although you may think the above quote has come from an American president, scholar, or revered business leader, this piece of timely advice emerged from the world of Harry Potter.

This is the hallmark of an internalized moral perspective. There will be many times when we face a tough choice. There is the easy road and then there is another, which requires far more self-determination and self-control.

Leaders can struggle with the weight of this responsibility. Here are some powerful reflection questions that can keep you aligned with your authentic leadership:

▶ What would your parent(s) think about the choice(s) you are about to make? How would

they advise you to approach the situation?
What elements would they emphasize and
de-emphasize in their advice?

▶ What would your employees/peers/supervisor/
stakeholders think about your decision? What
pieces of the puzzle would they feel are most
important?

▶ How would you feel if this decision were the
headline in your local or national newspaper?
How proud would you be about the feature
story? How defensible is your position?

▶ What advice would you provide to a fellow
executive if they were facing a similar situation?
What would you urge them to consider?

I would not be surprised if you read this set of questions and said, "Well, that's an idealistic and unrealistic
way to look at things. How can I possibly appease the
needs of each of these groups? Everyone will likely
have a different opinion."

Although this may surprise you, I agree with you!

The purpose of asking these questions is not to find
consensus. Rather, it is about considering each of these
points of view when making our decision. Although
these varying perspectives may not *change* our ultimate choice, they should *inform* it.

This is one of the primary reasons why research
has shown that empathetic leaders are also the most
ethical.[66] When they make decisions, they do not cave

or cater to one set of interests. On the contrary, they consider *all* sides and then frame their decision in a way that minimizes harm.

This is the ultimate expression of an internalized moral perspective.

CEO MASTERCLASS WITH ALAN MULALLY: ON MASTERING AUTHENTIC LEADERSHIP

The beauty of the "Working Together" Management System is not just in the extraordinary results it achieves; what makes it even more compelling is how authentic leadership plays an instrumental role. Rather than being seen as a complicating or inhibiting force, authentic leadership is viewed as critical to individual and collective success.

So what does it mean to exhibit authentic leadership? Here's Alan's definition: "Authentic leadership is when your values, your beliefs, and your behaviors are aligned. You don't act one way in one situation and totally differently in another. You are consistent regardless of who is there and what is happening."

The "Working Together" Principles and Practices are a powerful guidebook in terms of how we treat one another. "When these expected behaviors are clearly understood, we don't hold anything back."

Another critical element is enforced when "Working Together." "We never make a joke at someone else's expense," Alan says. "The reason is, it's never funny. Although people will 'go along to get along,' if they are concerned that they're going to be the butt of a joke or made fun of, it's going to make them think twice about whether they want to share their real situation. We need their honest insights. We need their authenticity. So we need an environment that absolutely treasures the way we treat each other so everyone can be authentic in their leadership and service."

Feelings can easily get hurt, especially when humor is involved, and even the most well-intentioned comment can have a painful impact under the surface. We can hold on to the memory of this hurt long after the event has passed.

Alan strongly believes that authentic leadership is also critical to building trust throughout the organization, especially with your direct reports. "The first questions people are going to ask you are, 'Who are you, really? What are your values? What are your beliefs? What do you stand for? Are you here for yourself, or are you here for the team/organization? Where are we going? What's our plan going forward? Do you see me?' They need answers to these questions so they can trust you and bring their best selves to work. And they're going to watch and see whether your behaviors match what you say. It's hard to fake that. You have to be authentic to get that right."

You may be thinking that "Working Together" is easy to do when you're succeeding as a team but are wondering what happens when times are tough. Alan has valuable insights: "The 'Working Together' Principles, Practices, and Management System is even more important when you're going through rough waters. When making a decision, you use it as your guiding light to see what it needs of you in any given moment. It ensures you stay consistent no matter what is going on. This is the heart of authentic leadership."

One of the most powerful benefits of authentic leadership is that it ensures people focus their energy on the right things. Alan says, "It's so much healthier to be at your best because you're not constantly thinking about how to 'look good.' You just focus on being who you really are and what you need to do, which is the magic of 'Working Together.'"

Protecting the "Working Together" Management System and the focus on authentic leadership is so important that it applies even when you have a superstar performer who is struggling to exhibit the expected behaviors. While many senior leaders and CEOs may be reluctant to confront these issues because of their fear of losing top talent, Alan emphasizes a different approach.

"Although we may love their skills and results," he cautions, "they can significantly degrade our collective performance because this is about people

'Working Together' to create value for all the stake-holders and the greater good. Because it's the synergy of all of us 'Working Together' that's going to make this happen, it's really important to have everybody committed to our 'Working Together' Principles, Practices, and Management System."

While a person may be struggling to follow "Working Together," this does not mean that we should immediately strong-arm them back in line or cast them aside. Alan says, "Make no mistake. It's a choice each person makes for themselves. We still love you and would love to help you move to following our commitment to our 'Working Together' Principles and Practices. We will get you a coach or give you any support you feel you need. But this is really your decision. We can't tell you what to do or make you do it, but these are the expectations of our working together."

Making sure the other person makes an authentic choice is critical for their benefit, as well as for the team. As Alan explains, "Once they make that decision, they're not going to let each other down, because they're not doing it for me. They're doing it because they believe in that compelling vision of 'Working Together' and our strategy and plan to achieve it."

CONCLUDING THOUGHTS

Despite the importance of leading authentically, it can be the ultimate challenge. To effectively accomplish this, we must understand ourselves in a profound and personal way, examining both the good and the bad. We must embrace the realities of our whole person to benefit from the unique talents and perspectives we bring to the world. Although it may be the ultimate leadership challenge, the rewards far exceed the effort. It is a journey we must approach with courage and passion every day!

A CHALLENGE

*Excellence is never an accident. It is always
the result of high intention, sincere effort
and intelligent execution; it represents the
wise choice of many alternatives—choice,
not chance, determines your destiny.*

—ARISTOTLE

The opening quote is a favorite of mine because it perfectly relates to the mastering of leadership that was set out in this book. The first step is to be highly intentional about our desire to get better at our craft. We must make this a part of our everyday living and leadership. It requires a foundation of purpose.

Although necessary, operating with intention is not enough. As the expression goes, "The road to hell is paved with good intentions." Mastering ourselves also requires *sincere* effort.

It's not about going through the motions. It is a passionate commitment to improve. It is about leaving everything we have on the floor.

Intention and effort set us up for success, but they do not guarantee it. As James Clear, bestselling author of *Atomic Habits*, so brilliantly and succinctly put it, "You do not rise to the level of your goals. You fall to the level of your systems." Intelligent execution is all about making sure you have systems in place that support the goals you set for yourself, your team, and your organization. Think about what you need to put in place to prevent you from falling short. Your aspirations will not carry you where you want to go; your systems and environment will.

The final part of the quote may also be the most important. How your leadership journey unfolds is determined by choice, not by chance. Whether and how you make it to your destination is entirely up to you.

Make no mistake. Being a leader is not easy. Our world is evolving in ways that will make this more, not less, of a challenge. Rather than see this as a problem, I see it as an immense opportunity. We can focus on rising to meet the challenge in front of us rather than falling to the pressures that accompany it.

This book has talked about why this is truly a time to lead. We have sifted through decades of leadership science and anecdotal evidence to craft a powerful business case for its importance and an action plan for its implementation. So what have we learned?

We must start with our mindset above all else. How we see the world and the expectations we put in place significantly alter and impact our realities. To achieve great things, it is essential to ask ourselves, *What is possible?* and to challenge our teams and our organizations to confront that question as well.

Our mindset is more fluid than we realize. Our personal beliefs and experiences combine to form our view of the world around us. It is imperative that we challenge ourselves to remain in growth mode. Recognize the triggers that can derail us and fight every day to maintain that level of focus and commitment.

Leadership is not just about thinking our way through things. It is about feeling our way as well. An equally important companion on our journey are the feelings we experience. They not only impact our energy, our relationships, and our accomplishments but also affect those we care about most.

To be most effective in mastering our emotions requires us to examine our feelings with the objectivity of a detective and the precision of a surgeon. We must approach understanding and managing our emotions as one of our top priorities. We can never stop learning. The path to our greatest successes comes from the unrelenting commitment to mastering our emotions.

Our ability to understand and manage our emotions also impacts our level of resilience. The world demands that we adjust and adapt to what comes our way. Recognizing that stress is not something done *to* us but done *by* us is a critical insight. It is imperative that we also identify and secure the resources we need to tackle the challenges we face.

Another lever we can pull is the unique talents we possess. Our strengths provide the key ingredients in our recipe for success and equip us with an invaluable set of tools to flourish throughout our time to lead. We must identify those gifts before we can fully leverage them.

Take the time for self-reflection and receiving external feedback about what makes us great. With that in hand, we next need to recognize how we can put our strengths to work for us. How can we leverage them to get the best out of ourselves and the people we lead? Finding ways of tapping into innate talents drives personal, team, and organizational engagement like nothing else.

At the same time, we cannot get complacent with our talents. Although they serve us well, we must not rest on our laurels. Mastering the art of receiving feedback well maximizes the chances we will not fall victim to our blind spots. It also provides a powerful pathway to deepen our relationships with others and for them to expand their appreciation of what we mean to them.

It is essential that we challenge ourselves to embrace the idea that feedback truly is the breakfast of champions, and it is not a solo endeavor. Although self-reflection can be useful, feedback is more balanced and healthier for us when it is an experience shared with everyone in our community of support, personally and professionally.

A special application and extension of the feedback principle is in navigating difficult conversations. These are a natural part of living and an expanded and critical part of leadership. One of the hallmarks reflecting our time to lead is how effectively we initiate and manage those conversations.

It takes a thoughtful and balanced approach. It requires us to think through many challenging questions. It denotes a commitment to finding a mutual path forward versus one that disproportionately advantages or disadvantages our interests. Navigating difficult conversations represents one of the most complex skills we can acquire, and the learning never stops.

Mastering authentic leadership was purposefully left for last, but not because it is the least important. Embracing authenticity and facilitating its expression in others is an essential part of mastering the fundamentals of leadership. Fully accepting and leading with aligned beliefs, values, and behaviors is the secret to profound success.

The Masterclasses featuring Alan Mulally are what tie all of this together so beautifully. They were a purposeful thread throughout this book so you could learn how one of the greatest CEOs leveraged each of the leadership qualities within his "Working Together" Principles, Practices, and Management System to extraordinary effect. As I reflect on the Masterclasses, what I personally love most is that Alan is talking about maximizing personal empowerment to maximize the benefits of "Working Together."

What brought Alan and me together and inspired countless conversations was our shared and unmistakable passion around the idea that knowing *who you need to be* and *what you need to do* are keys to mastering leadership.

Leadership is about doing good and making a difference—not just for ourselves but for others as well. It is the culmination of each of the chapters and Masterclasses covered in this book. It represents the highest manifestation of ourselves. It may be the scariest but most rewarding part of leadership.

The journey is not easy. It is about asking ourselves the tough questions. *Who are we? What do we believe in? What is most important to us? What impact do we want to make on the world? How do we need to behave?*

From there, we must take the even scarier step of living leadership. We must cast away from the safety of being who others want us to be and fully embrace the risks and rewards that come from being ourselves. Some days we will win that battle. Some days we will lose. The key is to keep going, committing to lifelong learning and continuous improvement.

IT'S YOUR TIME TO LEAD!

The fact that you made it to the end of this book reveals your desire to embrace your time to lead. Throughout these pages, my intention was to present an evidence-based roadmap for you to follow along with Masterclasses that provided real-life examples of these strategies in practice, led by a world-class CEO. The goal was not to share grandiose ideals and platitudes about leadership; it was to inspire you to recognize there is a powerful and actionable path forward—if you choose to take it.

Leadership is the ultimate responsibility that comes with ultimate rewards. It is an opportunity to truly test the limits of our potential. It is about bringing out the best in ourselves so we can do the same for others. It is about fully embracing who we are and who we want to become.

A couple of final thoughts. Don't take this journey alone. Invite others to come along for the ride. They may be with you for part of the way or for your entire adventure. Either way, you will learn from these experiences and deepen your practice and appreciation for your personal leadership.

The most beautiful and rewarding opportunity is to share our unique gifts with the world. There is no better way we can do this than to be the leaders we were destined to become. We wish you well on your journey. Thank you for inviting us to experience part of it with you. Remember to continue "Working Together" during your Time to Lead!

Acknowledgments

Although this is my second book, writing the acknowledgments doesn't get any easier. How can you possibly express appropriate gratitude to the countless individuals who so kindly provided their time, insights, and support? Please know that what I am about to write cannot fully capture the depth of my appreciation for each of you. For those whom I have missed, I hope you can forgive me.

Mom, you have been my earliest cheerleader and an incredible role model in my personal and professional life. Your desire to truly listen, support, and challenge me, through good times and bad, has been invaluable. We are more than mother and son. I am proud to call you my friend. Your undying love and encouragement mean the world to me.

My father was instrumental in instilling my work ethic. Through him, I learned the importance of committing to one's goals and leaving nothing on the floor to achieve them. I am grateful for those lessons.

To my sister, Dayna, and my "awesome nephews" Luke and Logan. I love spending time with you, and I can't wait to share more fun adventures very soon.

I would like to thank all my clients who have entrusted me with their leadership and organizational development. Working with dedicated and inspiring clients in the private, public, and nonprofit sectors is incredibly rewarding. I come away from every engagement for the better.

A special and heartfelt thank you to my collaborators, Alan Mulally and Sarah McArthur. I learned so much from our conversations and appreciated your support of this work. You were right that we would have so much fun "Working Together"! This is a highlight of my career with memories I will never forget.

During COVID-19, I launched the CEO Mastermind Forum. What started out as a small seed of an idea blossomed into a diverse and highly committed group of almost thirty high-integrity chief executives whose primary desires are to make their organizations and communities better places to work and live. They have inspired me with their passion and enriched me with their insights. I want to honor them alphabetically: Anil Arora (Chief Statistician of Canada), Horacio Barbeito (Walmart Canada), Tracey Black (Payments Canada), Charles Brown (LifeLabs), Lisa Calder (Canadian Medical Protective Association), Drew Collier (LGM Financial), Fred Dermarkar (Atomic Energy of Canada Limited), Eli Fathi (Mindbridge.ai), Kevin Ford (Calian

Group), Kim Furlong (Canadian Venture Capital and Private Equity Association), Michael Garrity (Financeit), Duane Green (Franklin Templeton Canada), Adam Hill (LGM Financial), Sue Hutchison (Equifax Canada), Nabeela Ixtabalan (Walmart Canada), Rob Paterson (Alterna Savings), Paul Preston (Genoa Design), Omar Salaymeh (Bonfire Interactive), Scott Tessier (Canada-Newfoundland Offshore Petroleum Board), Kathryn Tremblay (ExcelHR), Heather Tulk (Bioscript), Dan Turner (Xperigo), Mike Ward (IKEA Canada), Anne Whelan (Seafair Capital), and Kent Woodside (Porter Airlines).

My "Do Good to Lead Well" webinar series has been a continuous source of joy and inspiration. Although I cannot individually name every one of the 100-plus guests who have kindly shared their time and insights since its inception, a special thanks goes to the best-selling authors and TED speakers who joined me during the global pandemic. A warm thank you (in alphabetical order by last name) to: Teresa Amabile, Kim Cameron, Alexandra Carter, Doug Conant, Jim Detert, Chester Elton, Francesca Gino, Sally Helgesen, Ed Hess, Bryce Hoffman, Vicki Saunders, Barry Schwartz, Darryl Stickel, Margie Warrell, and Michele Zanini.

A couple of special mentions: Kim Cameron, the cofounder of the Center for Positive Organizations of the University of Michigan, has been incredibly kind with his support. Your enthusiasm for evidence-based positive leadership inspires me every day. You are beyond gracious in sharing your knowledge and time. I cannot thank you enough.

Ed Hess, the bestselling author of *Hyper-Learning* and *Humility Is the New Smart,* has also been an invaluable mentor. My enjoyment of our conversations has only been surpassed by what I have learned about the essence of human-centered leadership.

I feel very fortunate to know Marshall Goldsmith, the world's top-rated executive coach, who has influenced and inspired me since the beginning of my career. Your passion for coaching and for bringing out the best in people are second-to-none. Thank you, Marshall, for being the ultimate role model. "Life is good" every time I have the privilege of speaking with you.

Daniel Pink, you were foundational in informing my approach to my work and my career through your masterful integration of scientific research with actionable practice. No matter how busy your schedule is, you continually take time to respond in the kindest way. I am grateful you fully supported my mission statement, which I shamelessly adopted from your bestseller *Drive.* "My goal is to bridge the gap between what science knows and what leaders do." Daniel, thank you for continuing to be part of my journey!

I also appreciate the collaboration and friendship with Andrew Pardy and our launching of the Self-Aware Executive Program. I look forward to our continuing adventures.

An extra special thank you goes to my phenomenal book coach, Michael Levin. His advice and encouragement brought the best out of me, and I learned so much through this process. I am forever grateful our paths crossed, and I look forward to collaborating again on future books.

This book would not have been made possible without the support from Worth Books. A special thank-you is due to Justin Batt, who brought me into the fold. Your tireless commitment to delivering value, offering suggestions, and providing honest feedback has been integral to the final product. Jennifer Gingerich is also top-notch and kept me on track while exercising gentle persistence when my schedule was overflowing.

A very special acknowledgment goes to my new family. Although I may not be the first author to provide a shoutout to their pets, Crockett and Charley, my two English bulldogs, have brought immense joy and rich experiences to my life.

Allison and Lauren, thank you for welcoming me into your lives. I am grateful for the opportunity to get to know you, and I look forward to building more memories together.

Tara, I am so grateful the stars aligned and brought us together. You have brought incandescent love and laughter into my life. I cannot express how much our relationship means to me. I feel incredibly fortunate that we get to experience this amazing journey called life together. You're my best friend. I love you!

Meet My Collaborators

Alan Mulally

Alan Mulally served as president and chief executive officer of Ford Motor Company and was a member of Ford's board of directors from 2006 to 2014.

Mulally led Ford's transformation into one of the world's leading automobile companies and to its position as the #1 automobile brand in the United States. He guided Ford while working together on a compelling vision, comprehensive strategy, and implementation of the One Ford plan to deliver profitable growth for all the company's stakeholders.

Prior to joining Ford, Mulally served as executive vice president of Boeing, president and CEO of Boeing Commercial Airplanes, and president of Boeing Information, Space, and Defense Systems from 1969 to 2006.

Throughout his career, Mulally has been recognized for his contributions, industry leadership, and service, including being named #3 on *Fortune*'s "World's Greatest Leaders," one of the thirty "World's Best CEOs" by *Barron's*, one of "The World's Most influential

People" by *TIME*, "Chief Executive of the Year" by *Chief Executive* magazine, and Leader of the Future by the Frances Hesselbein Leadership Institute in 2006.

He was honored by the American Society for Quality with its medal for excellence in executive leadership as well as Automotive Executive of the Year and the Thomas Edison Achievement Award. Mulally is a Museum of Flight Pathfinder Award recipient and is a member of the Automobile Hall of Fame.

Mulally previously served on the President's Export Council under President Obama. He served as co-chairman of the Washington Competitiveness Council and has served on the advisory boards of the National Aeronautics and Space Administration, the University of Washington, the University of Kansas, Massachusetts Institute of Technology, and the Air Force Scientific Advisory Board. Mulally has also served as president of the American Institute of Aeronautics and Astronautics and as chairman of the Board of Governors of the Aerospace Industries Association. Mulally is a member of the United States National Academy of Engineering and a fellow of England's Royal Academy of Engineering.

Mulally currently serves on the board of directors of Google, Carbon 3D, and the Mayo Clinic.

Mulally holds bachelor's and master's of science degrees in aeronautical and astronautical engineering from the University of Kansas and earned a master's degree in management from Massachusetts Institute of Technology as an Alfred P. Sloan Fellow.

Sarah McArthur

Sarah McArthur is coeditor-in-chief of the *Leader to Leader* journal with Presidential Medal of Freedom recipient Frances Hesselbein and is a thought partner and trusted advisor to world-class leaders including former CEO of Boeing and Ford Alan Mulally, considered one of the greatest leaders of the 21st century. Her mission is to help leaders work together toward a bright future. Her fields of expertise include leadership, management, personal development, and executive and business coaching.

A writer, editor, and creative thought partner, Sarah has authored and edited many books including *Work Is Love Made Visible* with Marshall Goldsmith and Frances Hesselbein (foreword by Alan Mulally), and *Coaching for Leadership: Writings on Leadership from the World's Greatest Coaches* with Marshall Goldsmith and Laurence S. Lyons.

Former COO of Marshall Goldsmith Inc. from 2000 to 2020, Sarah managed the company's publishing ventures and daily operations and led many exciting initiatives. She played significant roles in the #1 *New York Times* and *Wall Street Journal* bestselling book *Triggers* and Goldsmith's Amazon.com, *USA Today*, and *Wall Street Journal* #1 bestseller *What Got You Here Won't Get You There*.

Currently she is an advisory board member of the Frances Hesselbein Leadership Forum in the Johnson Institute for Responsible Leadership at the University of

Pittsburgh's Graduate School of Public and International Affairs (GSPIA). Sarah is also a founding member of Marshall Goldsmith's 100 Coaches and 100 Coaches Europe and a certified Stakeholder Centered Coach.

Sarah graduated with a BA in English and environmental studies from the University of Oregon and a master's degree in publishing from George Washington University.

Notes

An Invitation

1 ESG is an increasingly common and supported set of metrics to assess the sustainability practices of companies. These nonfinancial metrics are also used by investors to identify potential risks and growth opportunities within these organizations.

2 Jamie Holmes, *Nonsense: The Power of Not Knowing.* (2015).

3 Ken Blanchard, "Feedback Is the Breakfast of Champions," *Ken Blanchard* (blog), August 17, 2009, https://www.kenblanchardbooks.com/feedback-is-the-breakfast-of-champions/.

Meet Your Co-Pilot

- "A Conversation with Alan Mulally about His "Working Together"© Strategic, Operational, and Stakeholder-Centered Management System," Alan Mulally and Sarah McArthur, *Leader to Leader*, Volume 104.

- *Twenty-First Century Jet: The Making and Marketing of the Boeing 777,* Book and Video, Karl Sabbagh.

- *American Icon: Alan Mulally and the Fight to Save Ford Motor Company*, Bryce Hoffman.

- *Work Is Love Made Visible: A Collection of Essays About the Power of Finding Your Purpose from the World's Greatest Thought Leaders*, Frances Hesselbein, Marshall Goldsmith, Sarah McArthur, foreword by Alan Mulally.

- *The Extraordinary Power of Leader Humility: Thriving*

Organizations - Great Results, foreword and chapter by Alan Mulally about how leader humility enables and nurtures effective working together by great teams, Marilyn Gist, PhD.

- "Working Together" Webinar, Alan Mulally Interview with Marshall Goldsmith, December 7, 2020.

Chapter 1: Mastering Our Mindset

4 Brian David Hodges. (2004) Medical student bodies and the pedagogy of self-reflection, self-assessment, and self-regulation. *Journal of Curriculum Theory, 20(2),* 41-51.

5 Joseph Saling, "What is the Placebo Effect?' *WebMD,* February 8, 2020, https://www.webmd.com/pain-management/what-is-the-placebo-effect

6 Hilke Plassmann, John O'Doherty, Baba Shiv, and Antonio Rangel (2008). "Marketing actions can modulate neural representations of experienced pleasantness." *Proceedings of the National Academy of Sciences* 105 (3) 1050-1054

7 Plassmann, O'Doherty, Shiv, and Rangel, "Marketing actions can modulate neural representations of experienced pleasantness."

8 Plassmann, O'Doherty, Shiv, and Rangel, "Marketing actions can modulate neural representations of experienced pleasantness."

9 For readers who are looking for a comprehensive and in-depth examination of this invaluable body of work research, please check out her bestselling book: Carol Dweck. *Mindset: The New Psychology of Success.* (2007).

10 Lisa Trei. "Fixed Versus Growth Intelligence Mindsets: It's All in Your Head, Dweck Says." *Stanford News Release,* February 7, 2007, https://news.stanford.edu/pr/2007/pr-dweck-020707.html#:~:text=According%20to%20Dweck%2C%20people%27s%20self,mistakes%20and%20not%20look%20smart.

11 Christine Gross-Loh, "How Praise Became a Consolation Prize." *The Atlantic,* December 16, 2016. https://www.theatlantic.com/education/archive/2016/12/how-praise-became-a-consolation-prize/510845/

12 Christine Gross-Loh, "How Praise Became a Consolation Prize."

13 Chapter 5 will make that very point and cover how we can receive it most effectively.

14 Victor Lipman, "66% of Employees Would Quit if They Feel Unappreciated," *Forbes*, April 15, 2017, https://www.forbes.com/sites/victorlipman/2017/04/15/66-of-employ-ees-would-quit-if-they-feel-unappreciated/?sh=5d58003a6897.

15 Carol Dweck, "What Having a 'Growth Mindset' Actually Means," *Harvard Business Review*, January 13, 2016, https://hbr.org/2016/01/what-having-a-growth-mindset-actually-means.

16 Carol Dweck, "What Having a 'Growth Mindset' Actually Means."

17 Dweck, *Mindset*.(page 55)

18 Dweck, *Mindset*. (page 56)

19 Check out *The CEO Test* by bestselling author Adam Bryant to learn more about this case example. Adam wrote the Corner Office column for *The New York Times* and played an integral role in this turnaround story.

20 "Building a Digital *New York Times*: CEO Mark Thompson," McKinsey & Company, August 10, 2020, https://www.mckinsey.com/industries/technology-media-and-telecommunications/our-insights/building-a-digital-new-york-times-ceo-mark-thompson.

Chapter 2: Mastering Our Emotions

21 While most people use the terms *emotions*, *feelings*, and *moods* interchangeably, researchers from the University of West Alabama argue this is incorrect. According to their work, "feelings arise from an emotional experience [and] a feeling is the result of an emotion." Moods, however, "differ from emotions because they lack stimuli and have no clear starting point."

22 American Psychological Association - Dictionary of Psychology. Accessed online April 14, 2022. https://dictionary.apa.org/emotion

23 Jared B. Torre and Matthew D. Lieberman, "Putting Feelings into Words: Affect Labeling as Implicit Emotion Regulation,"

Emotion Review 10, no. 2 (2018): 116–24.

24 Amelia Aldao, "Why Labeling Emotions Matters," *Psychology Today*, August 4, 2014, https://www.psychologytoday.com/ca/blog/sweet-emotion/201408/why-labeling-emotions-matters.

25 "That Giant Tarantula Is Terrifying, but I'll Touch It: Expressing Your Emotions Can Reduce Fear," *Science Daily*, September 4, 2012, https://www.sciencedaily.com/releases/2012/09/120904192045.htm.

26 "That Giant Tarantula Is Terrifying."

27 "That Giant Tarantula Is Terrifying."

28 Lucas S. LaFreniere and Michelle G. Newman, "Exposing Worry's Deceit: Percentage of Untrue Worries in Generalized Anxiety Disorder Treatment," *Behavior Therapy*, 51(3) (2020): 413–423.

29 New York Times Archives, "Don't Worry! There Is A Way," *The New York Times*, July 15, 1986).

30 Rui Fan, Ke Xu, and Jichang Zhao, "Easier Contagion and Weaker Ties Make Anger Spread Faster than Joy in Social Media," ResearchGate, August 15, 2016, https://www.researchgate.net/publication/306186965_Easier_contagion_and_weaker_ties_make_anger_spread_faster_than_joy_in_social_media.

31 Jennifer Lerner, Ye Li, Piercarlo Valdesolo, and Karim Kassam, "Emotion and Decision Making," *Annual Review of Psychology*, 66(1), 799-823.

Chapter 3: Mastering Our Resilience

32 This notion of a biological set point has also been discovered in other areas, including happiness and emotional intelligence.

33 Aviva Berkovich-Ohana, Meytal Wilf, Roni Kahana, Amos Arieli, and Rafael Malach, "Repetitive Speech Elicits Widespread Deactivation in the Human Cortex: The 'Mantra' Effect?," *Brain Behavior* 5, no. 7 (2015): e00346.

34 Kelly McGonigal, *The Upside of Stress*. (2016).

35 A valuable acronym for FEAR is False Evidence Appearing Real. It shows the psychological phenomenon of how we can be afraid

of future events that may never happen. When we are fearful
of something happening, a powerful exercise is to examine the
evidence we have to support it. Often, it is much more emotion-
than fact-based.

Chapter 4: Mastering Our Strengths

36 "What Is the Difference Between a Talent and a Strength?,"
CliftonStrengths for Students, https://towson.gallup.com/help/
general/273908/difference-talent-strength.aspx.

37 Jack Zenger and Joseph Folkman, "Bad Leaders Can Change
Their Spots," *Harvard Business Review*, January 24, 2013,
https://hbr.org/2013/01/good-news-poor-leaders-can-cha.

38 Roy F. Baumeister, Ellen Bratslavsky, Catrin Finkenauer, and
Kathleen D. Vohs, "Bad Is Stronger than Good," *Review of
General Psychology* 5, no. 4 (2001): 323–370.

39 Jack Zenger, *Developing Strengths or Weaknesses*, Zenger
Folkman, https://zengerfolkman.com/wp-content/
uploads/2019/08/Developing-Strengths-or-Weaknesses_
WP-2019.pdf.

40 "The VIA Character Strengths Survey," VIA Institute on
Character, https://www.viacharacter.org/account/register.

Chapter 5: Mastering Receiving Feedback

41 "Feedback: The Leadership Practice That Needs Elevating for
the Hybrid Workforce," Zenger Folkman, February 10, 2022,
https://zengerfolkman.com/articles/feedback-the-leadership-
practice-that-needs-elevating-for-the-hybrid-workforce/.

42 Andrew Mauboussin and Michael J. Mauboussin, " If You
Say Something Is 'Likely,' How Likely Do People Think It Is?,"
Harvard Business Review, https://hbr.org/2018/07/if-you-say-
something-is-likely-how-likely-do-people-think-it-is.

43 Zenger, *Developing Strengths or Weaknesses*.

44 Douglas Stone and Sheila Heen, *Thanks for the Feedback: The
Science and Art of Receiving Feedback Well* (2015).

Chapter 6: Mastering Difficult Conversations

45 Joseph Grenny, Kerry Patterson, Ron McMillan, Al Switzler, and Emily Gregory, *Crucial Conversations: Tools for Talking When Stakes Are High* (2021).

46 "Ladder of Inference," Harvard Law School, February 17, 2009, https://www.pon.harvard.edu/glossary/ladder-of-inference/.

47 Dorie Clark, "If Strategy Is So Important, Why Don't We Make Time for It?," *Harvard Business Review*, June 21, 2018, https://hbr.org/2018/06/if-strategy-is-so-important-why-dont-we-make-time-for-it.

48 William Ury, *The Power of a Positive No: How to Say No and Still Get to Yes* (2007).

Chapter 7: Mastering Authentic Leadership

49 Susan M. Jensen and Fred Luthans, "Entrepreneurs as Authentic Leaders: Impact on Employees' Attitudes," *Leadership & Organization Development Journal* 27, no. 8 (2006).

50 Mariola Laguna, Karolina Walachowska, Marjan Gorgievski, and Juan Moriano, "Authentic Leadership and Employee Innovative Behaviour: A Multilevel Investigation in Three Countries," *International Journal of Environmental Research and Public Health* 16, no. 21 (2019): 4201.

51 Qaiser Mehmood, Samina Nawab, and Melvyn R. W. Hamstra, "Does Authentic Leadership Predict Employee Work Engagement and In-Role Performance? Considering the Role of Learning Goal Orientation," *Journal of Personnel Psychology* 15, no. 3 (2016).

52 Suzanne Peterson, Fred O. Walumbwa, Bruce J. Avolio, and Sean T. Hannah, "The Relationship Between Authentic Leadership and Follower Job Performance: The Mediating Role of Follower Positivity in Extreme Contexts," *The Leadership Quarterly*, 23(3), 502-516.

53 Hui Wang, Yang Sui, Fred Luthans, Danni Wang, and Yanhong Wu, "Impact of Authentic Leadership on Performance: Role of Followers' Positive Psychological Capital and Relational Processes," *Journal of Organizational Behavior* 35, no. 1

(January 2014): 5–21.

54 Arif Hassan and Frobis Ahmed, "Authentic Leadership, Trust and Work Engagement," *International Journal of Economics and Management Engineering* 5, no. 8 (2011): 1036–42.

55 "Diversity & Inclusion Require Authentic Leadership, Says New Research," Benedictine University, June 6, 2016, https://cvdl. ben.edu/blog/diversity-inclusion-require-authentic-leadership-research/.

56 Anna Powers, "A Study Finds That Diverse Companies Produce 19% More Revenue," *Forbes*, June 27, 2018, https://www.forbes. com/sites/annapowers/2018/06/27/a-study-finds-that-diverse-companies-produce-19-more-revenue/?sh=4eabca09506f; "Diversity Wins: How Inclusion Matters," McKinsey & Company, May 19, 2020, https://www.mckinsey.com/featured-insights/ diversity-and-inclusion/diversity-wins-how-inclusion-matters; "Diversity & Inclusion Require Authentic Leadership."

57 Vanessa Buote, "Most Employees Feel Authentic at Work, but It Can Take a While," *Harvard Business Review*, May 11, 2016, https://hbr.org/2016/05/most-employees-feel-authentic-at-work-but-it-can-take-a-while.

58 F. O. Walumbwa, B. J. Avolio, W. L. Gardner, T. S. Wernsing, and S. J. Peterson, "Authentic Leadership: Development and Validation of a Theory-Based Measure," *Journal of Management* 34, no. 1 (2008): 89–126.

59 Brené Brown, *The Gifts of Imperfection* (2020).

60 Adam Grant, "Unless You're Oprah, 'Be Yourself' Is Terrible Advice," *The New York Times*, June 4, 2016, https://www. nytimes.com/2016/06/05/opinion/sunday/unless-youre-oprah-be-yourself-is-terrible-advice.html.

61 "Bill George: Authentic Leadership and Letting Your Strengths 'Bloom,'" Wharton School of Business, July 15, 2014, http:// knowledge.wharton.upenn.edu/article/authentic-leadership/.

62 Bill George, "HBS: The Truth About Authentic Leaders," Bill George, July 6, 2016, http://www.billgeorge.org/articles/ hbs-the-truth-about-authentic-leaders/.

63 George, "HBS: The Truth About Authentic Leaders."

64 Travis Bradberry, *Self-Awareness* (2009).
65 Research conducted by Korn Ferry showed that executive teams comprised of members who possessed higher levels of self-awareness experienced significant benefits, including a higher bottom line.
66 It is also important to note that the same research uncovered that empathy is also one of the top three significant predictors of executive excellence. https://financialpost.com/executive/c-suite/forget-ethics-training-focus-on-empathy.

How do you lead successfully while living your values?

Answering that question is at the heart of Craig Dowden's first book, *Do Good to Lead Well: The Science and Practice of Positive Leadership*, where he explores the six pillars of positive leadership.

Learn more about Craig Dowden at
www.CraigDowden.com.